Emanoel Lee

TO THE BITTER END

A Photographic History of

the Boer War 1899-1902

VIKING

VIKING

Penguin Books Ltd, Harmondsworth, Middlesex, England
Viking Penguin Inc., 40 West 23rd Street, New York, New York 10010, U.S.A.
Penguin Books Australia Ltd, Ringwood, Victoria, Australia
Penguin Books Canada Ltd, 2801 John Street, Markham, Ontario, Canada L3R 1B4
Penguin Books (N.Z.) Ltd, 182-190 Wairau Road, Auckland 10, New Zealand

First published 1985

Copyright © Emanoel Lee, 1985

Typeset in 10/12 Sabon

Printed in Great Britain by
Butler & Tanner Ltd, Frome and London

British Library Cataloguing in Publication Data
Lee, Emanoel C.G.
    To the bitter end: a photographic history
    of the Boer War 1899-1902.
    1. South African War, 1899-1902
    I. Title
    968.04'8   DT930

    ISBN 0-670-80143-7

Library of Congress Catalog Card Number: 84-52345

TO JAN, RUBEN AND PAUL,

FOR YEARS OF

ENCOURAGEMENT AND HELP

CONTENTS

LIST OF MAPS

PREFACE

I am happy to write a preface to this remarkable book. The Boer War is a fascinating subject – Britain's Vietnam, as it has been described, though the parallel should not be pressed too closely, for after all Britain did in the end win, whereas the Americans lost. The idea of producing a photographic history of this strange campaign is an original one, and on the face of things might seem unpromising. In fact Mr Lee has been immensely successful. There had been war photography before; the earliest was in the Mexican war of 1840, and the best was the superb photographic record of the campaign in the Crimea. This was the work of professionals, who, oddly enough, were much less successful in South Africa. The change which had occurred in the 1890s was the invention of the Eastman Kodak camera, which any amateur could handle; followed in 1900 by the even simpler Brownie. The number of soldiers and civilians who used these in South Africa during the war is unknown, but, as Mr Lee says, must have run into thousands. Most of the illustrations in this book are taken from personal albums and have not been published till now. The quality is remarkably high, and, within limits imposed by the medium, they throw fresh light on history.

Mr Lee's account of the war is scrupulously fair and objective. He rightly gives proper emphasis to its closing stages, which tend to be skimped by British writers. Some of the best photographs illustrate this period. He is extremely interesting on the medical aspects – the treatment of wounds, the effects of diseases like typhoid and malaria, and the terrible story of the concentration camps where over 25,000 died, for the most part women and children. This mortality was not the result of malice or neglect. The inmates of the camps were not short of food. Doctors simply did not know about vitamins or community resistance to disease, and the situation was made worse by the bitterest winter for a hundred years. What occurred was not a crime, but one can hardly wonder that it has been viewed as such by the Afrikaners ever since, with effects on relations with Britain which still reverberate today.

Robert Blake

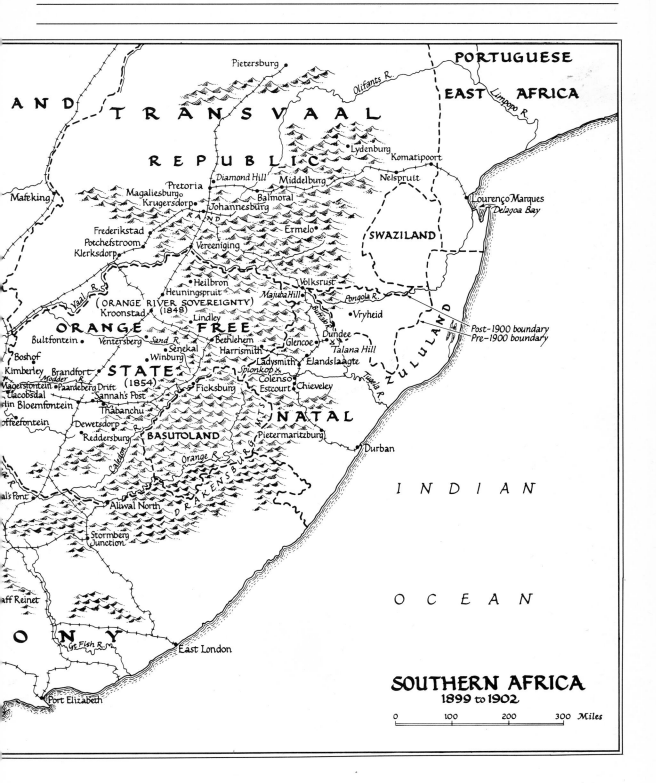

SOUTHERN AFRICA
1899 to 1902

0   100   200   300 *Miles*

ACKNOWLEDGEMENTS

Too many people have helped in the collection of photographs and data used in preparing this book for all to be named, but particular thanks are due to Lord Methuen, Mr Anthony Speyer, and Professor Richard Cobb of Worcester College, Oxford, for allowing me to use photographs from family collections.

I would also like to thank Mr N.L. Schwartz for his catalytic action, Mrs Barbara Kaufman, Mrs Jane Carlow and Mrs Brenda Carter for all their work on the manuscript, and Pamela and Philip Joseph for their hard work and expertise.

I am grateful for help received from the directors and staff of the War Museum of the Boer Republic, Bloemfontein, South Africa; the National Library of Ireland and the National Museum of Ireland, Dublin; the National Army Museum, Chelsea; the Kodak Museum, Hendon; and the George Eastman Museum, Rochester, New York; and from Mr Frank Brownell Mehlenbacher, grandson of George Eastman's camera-maker.

Finally I would like to thank Mr D.K. Smurthwaite of the National Army Museum, Mr Brian Coe of the Kodak Museum, and Lord Blake, Provost of The Queen's College, Oxford, for reading the manuscript and offering most helpful advice.

INTRODUCTION

"30 CHILDREN HURT IN SCHOOL EXPLOSION"

PLAYGROUND DETONATION AT CROSBY: TEACHER INJURED

More than 30 children and a schoolteacher, Mr A.F. Knoetze, were injured when what may have been a mortar bomb exploded in the playground of the Crosby Afrikaans-medium school at 11 a.m. today. The bomb exploded as the children were coming out of the classroom. The bomb is believed to have been brought to the school by one of the children, who is now lying in hospital with serious leg injuries. In the classroom he showed the bomb to his teacher who told him not to play with it as it was dangerous. As the class came out the bomb either fell from his grasp or was thrown to the ground where it exploded.

HIT BY SPLINTERS

The teacher who was injured ... is said to have been standing 50 yards from the scene of the explosion. He was hit in the legs by splinters.

Children who saw the bomb describe it as being rusty and from six to eight inches long. It is not yet known how the children came into possession of the bomb, but the police are investigating a report that it was found lying on the school rugby field."

This report appeared on the front page of the *Star*, a Johannesburg newspaper, on 9 March 1953. It was followed by a list of the children's names and injuries. The boy who found the bomb, Jacobus Jordaan, was carried into the Casualty Department of the hospital with his shattered feet dangling in front of him. Behind came a mob of people carrying the other injured children. In a moment the quiet hall became a scene of war.

As a young medical student, new to clinical work, I had been trying to work up enough courage to watch a nurse give an injection. In those days the world was not used to daily bomb attacks. The impact of the events of the next six hours has not lessened over the years. One detail still stands out with great clarity: the vision of a surgeon with war experience, Mr Joss Lannon, assuming command and converting chaos into order.

Subsequently the Chief Inspector of Explosives carefully pieced together the fragments and found that the 'bomb' was a three-pound British shell which had been manufactured in 1901. It had been found on a koppie near the school, where it had lain for more than fifty years. We had witnessed the last engagement of the Anglo-Boer War. During the months that followed I searched my home town for other evidence of the conflict; apart from an old cannon or two standing in front of public buildings, I found surprisingly little.

But physical evidence does exist, evidence which no previous war had ever left behind in such quantity – the photographs of the period. Over the years I have searched both South Africa and England for them. This book is the result of that search. Its structure grew from the records themselves, its character from the realization that the photographs were throwing light on to the last phase of the war, which most recent authors have not emphasized sufficiently, concentrating instead on the formal battles of the first few months. But it was not even the change in character of the fighting which became for me the central interest of the war: the photographs also led me to examine its medical aspects in detail. It is on this feature of the guerilla war, which has had the most lasting consequences in South Africa, that the book focuses.

To interpret the war as a typical nineteenth-century campaign in which large forces engaged in set battles is to ignore the last eighteen months of fighting, when sporadic and apparently unconnected engagements took place all over the country. It was not simply a 'mopping up' or 'guerilla' campaign. To the end, the Boers retained a formal army which constantly co-ordinated the attacks of widely dispersed units, and which had a definite strategic policy. Such a campaign is much more difficult to write about than one of set battles which can be described sequentially. This closing phase of the war becomes comprehensible when seen as a gigantic chess-game in which both sides made tactical and strategic moves and counter-moves.

However, for me it was not enough merely to understand what happened. To satisfy a doctor's craving to get to grips with the nature of personal experience, I needed something more than the written word. Here the photographs proved to be much more exciting than I had anticipated, especially those taken by amateurs. Many of the pictures used in this book are from my own collection; the majority have never been published. However, the book is not merely a compilation of photographs. It has been designed to contain a mixture of written and visual images. My task has been to match the images with the historical documents. It is hoped that the juxtaposition will produce in the reader a sharpened sense of reality.

But let us for a moment separate the pictures from the words and explain why it was that, for the first time in history, the very

1. Boer artillery with photographer using a full-plate camera.

soldiers who fought in the war had access to the camera. Although not the first campaign to be photographed, the Boer War coincided with many of the technical advances on which modern photography is based. Professional photographers had been active in most hostilities since daguerreotypes were taken of the Mexican War in the 1840s, but Roger Fenton's marvellous pictures from the Crimea were the first serious photographic record of a military campaign.

The Crimean photographs attracted so much attention that magazines such as the *Illustrated London News* published engraved copies. In the American Civil War, photographers such as Mathew Brady produced work which has never been surpassed. The Victorian public soon developed an insatiable interest in photography. At a very early stage they were used extensively in books and magazines. Fox-Talbot himself patented a method of reproduction which allowed photographs to be printed from steel plates, but this was crude. In 1866 Woodbury devised a printing technique using lead plates. Prints made with his process are amongst the best copies of photographs produced until very recent

times, but the lead plates were too soft to be used in a high-speed printing press, so that the prints had to be made separately and pasted laboriously into spaces left for them. In the 1880s the half-tone process was perfected. It allowed tough metal plates to be made and fitted into the standard blocks used by commercial printers. There was an immediate explosion of cheap picture magazines. It is possible that the wide use of photographs and illustrations was partly responsible for the rising popularity of newspapers at the time.

When the Boer War began there were many successful photographic magazines and a host of new ones sprang up solely to report the fighting. Many hired their own photographers. Most cameras were large and difficult to use, but in the 1880s a number of hand cameras were brought out. These were simply modifications of the studio tripod and used dry-plate glass negatives, a process introduced by Dr Maddox in 1871. However, their achromatic lenses and shutter mechanisms allowed rapid exposures to be made with high-speed emulsions. Exposed plates could be kept for some time before developing, but they were fragile and had to be encased in heavy plate-holders.

Most professional photographs of the war are of excellent quality but curiously stilted. One reason was the difficulty of getting close to the fighting. The effective range of a rifle far out-distanced that of a camera. Although a few telephoto lenses were taken to Africa, they were not very successful: they could compress the foreground and background into focus and enlarge distant objects, but were still not good enough to get clear close-up shots. The photo-journalist H.C. Shelley described the difficulties of war photography in a series of articles published in the magazine *Amateur Photographer*, He discussed the use of the telephoto lens and even described reconnaissance pictures taken from war balloons. His equipment included Kodak cameras, which he rarely used because he was unable to find suitable enlargers in Africa to print their small negatives. Like most professionals, he far preferred full- or half-plate cameras which made excellent negatives for contact printing.

In the Boer War no professional produced work to compare with the pictures of the Crimea and the American Civil War. It was a failure of style rather than equipment. Most photographers had been trained before the introduction of high-speed materials. They arranged scenes into pictures which combined the disadvantages of a static image with great clarity of detail. The crude strength of their predecessor's images was replaced by innumerable distant panoramas with frozen groups of men in the foreground. Close-ups were virtually never taken outside the studio. The dead were hardly ever photographed. Their war-images seem embalmed in nineteenth-century heroic rhetoric. This was true of

2. 'The Worcesters charging a Kopje and facing death near Norval's Pont.' An obviously posed stereoscopic battle photograph in the Underwood series.

The Worcesters charging a Kopje and facing death near Norval's Pont, South Africa. Copyright Underwood & Underwood.

most newspaper reports as well as the photographs. Stereoscopic photographs of an 'engagement' show 'dead soldiers' draped carefully over suitable rocks. There are no signs of injury and in the heat the veins of their dangling arms stand out sharply in three dimensions, full of living blood flowing back to a beating heart. There is no shock, no blood, no sweat. Photo-realism lay far in the future. People were not yet trained to stand the realities of war. Journalists were mainly interested in getting a record of who was there.

A number of photographic innovations caused excitement at the time. Two American brothers, the Underwoods, hit on the idea of employing door-to-door salesmen to sell collections of stereoscopic photographs of the war. The sets were issued in boxes made to look like a pair of books entitled 'The South African War through the Stereoscope', containing 150 photographs pasted on cardboard. More and more titles were added as the war went on, and it is now rare to find two boxes containing the same set of pictures. The Underwoods hired their own photographers, some of whom were Americans. Unfortunately their names are not recorded on the cards. Photographs were also bought from the Boer side. These are rare. It is not even known how many photographs or sets were made. The negatives were sold later to the Keystone firm, which reissued some of the titles. The Underwood originals have a rich sepia tone, although some have faded; Keystone prints are much darker. Until recently the Underwood copyright was owned by a New York firm. The last owner told me that he knew of more than 3,000 photographs of the war sold under the Underwood label. He died recently and the collection was broken up. The pictures of most historical interest are the portraits. To see the young Churchill startingly alive in three dimensions is a delight.

Potentially the most important development was the movie newsreel. In 1896, Casler of New York patented the 'Biograph' equipment in which large-frame film was moved through the special camera or projector by rollers rather than sprockets. The bigger negatives and rapid speed improved the projection quality and reduced flickering. A company was formed to photograph historical events, and a team of cameramen was sent out to South Africa with General Buller. They took pictures of him, and of troops marching. There also exists film of horse-drawn guns, a cavalry charge, a troop train, and a number of battle scenes. Most of the Biograph movies were obviously staged and were probably not even in Africa, though one of the cameramen, Dickson, published a book called *The Biograph in Battle in the South African War*. The films were shown throughout the world to excited audiences. As the first 'movies' of war, they set the public taste for the newsreels which became such a feature of the First World War. The quality of individual frames is poor, and no prints from Biograph film have been used in this book.

Finally we come to the most important photographic development of that period: for the first time it was possible for everyone to use a camera. The change was brought about almost single-handed by an American photographic glass-plate manufacturer, George Eastman of Rochester, who was certainly a business genius. He saw clearly the enormous market for simple cameras which ordinary people could handle. His first step was to design, with William Walker, a holder which could adapt a plate-camera to take rolls of light-sensitive paper. This was put on sale in 1885. Three years later he introduced a camera incorporating the holder. Searching for a trade-name pronounceable in most languages, he decided on the word 'Kodak'. The first Kodak camera designed for roll-film was of a simple box type. Each film took 100 circular exposures 2.5 inches in diameter. It was specifically made for amateur use. All the photographer had to do was to cock the

3. The first Kodak camera (brought out in 1896) with a box of roll film.

shutter by pulling a string, aim the camera using 'sighting lines' on the top, and press the button. The film was wound on with a key. A book was sold with the camera to record what had been taken. When the film was exposed, the camera was returned by post to Eastman's factory, where it was unloaded, reloaded with fresh film and returned with the printed photographs. In America the whole operation took ten days. Eastman soon set up a world service. The development and printing service was the most revolutionary part of his idea. 'You press the button, we do the rest.' But it was not cheap. Cameras cost five guineas in England, and the processing of each film cost two guineas.

Eastman was immediately successful; the firm expanded rapidly and he arranged for Frank A. Brownell, a Rochester manufacturer, to make the Kodak cameras. Brownell's grandson, Frank Brownell Mehlenbacher, has a letter from Eastman dated 21 June 1898, explaining that, although their original agreement had guaranteed Brownell 10 per cent of the yearly profit, sales had been so large that he proposed to limit Brownell's subsequent profits to 5 per cent. It seems not to have caused a rift between them. During the next few years a succession of different cameras were introduced.

The first films were made by coating a roll of paper with a gelatin emulsion; later films had paper acting simply as a temporary support for the gelatin. However, prints made with these paper 'films' were not as clear as those produced by glass negatives. Eastman hired a chemist, Henry Reichenbach, to produce a flexible material as transparent as glass. The paper backing was soon discarded when Reichenbach adopted the new transparent material, cellulose nitrate, called 'celluloid'. The new film was patented and introduced in 1889. Within three years Eastman was selling it for all his new cameras. It was a breakthrough. Amateur photographers were now able to take high-quality pictures, and other camera makers all over the world began to manufacture roll-film cameras.

More improvements followed. In 1891 Eastman introduced three sizes of 'Day-light' cameras, which could be loaded at home. They used rolls of celluloid film with strips of black cloth on paper attached to both ends. The film was fitted in a cardboard carton with velvet edged light-traps, like the modern 35 mm cassette. The film could be loaded in daylight using the black 'leader'. In the camera it was wound from one carton to another, but Eastman was not satisfied with the cartons. In 1895 he acquired the rights to a patent in which the film was fitted in a larger roll of black paper. This protected it from light when wound on a spool. Numbers printed on the back of the paper were visible through a red window on the back of the camera, so that exposures were taken at the correct distance from each other.

The first cameras to use 'cartridge film' (still in use today), were

4 (*below left*). No. 1 Folding Pocket Kodak camera, in use between 1897 and 1904. Many of the photographs in British troops' albums were taken with this model.

5 (*right*). The first Brownie Kodak camera cost five shillings. The viewer was bought separately for sixpence.

6 (*below*). An Elswick gun in action. The photograph was taken with a Panoram camera which produced a very wide view with a rotating lens.

8

the Pocket and Bullet Kodaks. The Folding Pocket camera was tiny, taking pictures only 1.5 by 2 inches in size. It cost one guinea and was the first camera to be mass-produced. In 1896 the Bullseye camera was made for the professional market. It took square pictures 3.5 inches in size. Two years later a much larger folding camera called the Cartridge Kodak was released for the same market. It was eventually sold in three sizes, taking pictures 5 by 7 inches, 5 by 4 inches and 3.75 by 4.25 inches. The cameras were built to a high standard of craftsmanship, their interiors being constructed of wood and brass. Another specialized camera was the Panoram Kodak, whose swivelling lens enabled it to take very wide views. It came in two sizes, producing photographs 3.5 by 12 inches and 2.25 by 7 inches, and was available in England from 1900. Quite a number of Boer War photographs seem to have been taken with these instruments, and collectors are often able to tell by the size of the pictures which camera was used.

In 1900 Eastman brought out the first Brownie camera, aimed at developing a children's market. It was very cheap, the price in England being five shillings with two rolls of film. As an optional extra, a view-finder could be clipped on for a shilling. It took

7. Brownie snap from late in the guerilla war of a British officer with his essential equipment: an Australian hat and a camera.

pictures 2.25 inches square. The camera was made in large numbers from wood and cardboard covered with a black material simulating leather. It looked like a toy but could take remarkably good pictures. Some of the original ones can still be used. A succession of different sizes and models appeared year after year until the Second World War. When the patents expired, camera-makers all over the world copied the basic design.

Between 1898 and 1902 nearly 60,000 Folding Pocket Kodak cameras were sold outside America. The Brownie was even more successful. Between 1900, when it was introduced, and the end of the Boer War, nearly 150,000 Brownies were sold in the same market. For the first time it was possible for amateurs to take photographs easily and cheaply, without learning how to develop and print. To the Brownie camera and the roll-film can rightly be ascribed the start of popular photography.

By the end of the Boer War nearly 400,000 British and Colonial troops had visited South Africa. No one knows how many soldiers were interested enough (or could afford) to bring a camera, but the number must have run into thousands. The war was the main exciting event to coincide with the Brownie coming on to the market. Kodak cameras and film were used by most of the amateurs who photographed it, and because of the careful patents taken

8. The quality of amateur photography in 1902: enlargement of a Brownie snap taken late in the war and found among campaign photographs in a British officer's album. The sitters are unknown.

out by Eastman, even British and European cameras were designed to use Kodak roll-film. Eastman's innovations caused not only a revolution in photographic technique, but an entirely new view of history. At almost every important event since that time, someone has had a camera ready cocked. There were so many enthusiasts about that no one took much notice of them and posing became less common. Although photo-journalists learned quickly, Boer War amateur snaps are often of greater historical significance than the official photographs. They are also of a surprising quality: the amateur photographers were lucky in having enormous help from the strong South African sunlight.

This book is in part dedicated to Eastman. The majority of its illustrations have been made from photographs taken with his equipment by amateurs. They provide a new and, I feel, a more accurate vision of events. Most of these photographs come from personal albums, and very few have been seen by the general public. Still more have been destroyed or lie in family attics. It is one of the purposes of this book to point out their historical significance, so that those which remain may be saved. However, the final image which has been salvaged from the past is still a limited one: the pictures do not capture the colour and grandeur of the African landscape, nor do they show everything that happened. What we have is all that could be captured in a little black box, but it is enough to give a taste of reality.

Left to right

General Sir Redvers H.
Buller, first Commander-
in-Chief in South Africa
(1899).

Field Marshal Lord
Roberts of Kandahar,
who replaced Buller as
Commander-in-Chief
in December 1899.

General Lord Kitchener
of Khartoum, assistant to
Lord Roberts. He became
Commander-in-Chief
when Roberts left South
Africa in 1900.

General Sir W. Penn
Symons, killed at the
Battle of Dundee (1899).

Left to right

Lieutenant-General Lord Methuen, commander of British forces in the Cape during Buller's campaign.

General J.D.P. French, commander of the Cavalry Division in South Africa.

Lieutenant-General Sir W.F. Gatacre, who was responsible for the reverse at Stormberg Junction during 'Black Week'.

Major-General A.G. Wauchope, killed at the Battle of Magersfontein (1899).

Colonel R.S.S. Baden-
Powell, who became
famous for his defence of
Mafeking during the siege.

Photographs from the author's
collection

Stephanus Johannes
Paulus Kruger, President
of the Transvaal
Republic.

Left to right

Commandant-General
Petrus Jacobus Joubert,
Commander-in-Chief of
the Boer forces in 1899.

Commandant-General
Louis Botha, who
replaced Joubert as
Commander-in-Chief in
December 1899.

General Jacobus
Herculaas de la Rey of
the Transvaal, who
introduced important
changes in commando
tactics.

General Christiaan Rudolf
de Wet, Commander-in-
Chief of the Orange Free
State Commandos during
the guerilla campaign.

Marthinus Theunis Steyn
(in black top hat),
President of the Orange
Free State Republic.

Photographs courtesy of the
Africana Museum, Johannesburg;
the Boer War Museum,
Bloemfontein; and the Transvaal
State Archives, Pretoria

1. BACKGROUND TO THE WAR

Serious fighting between British colonial territories in Southern Africa and the Boer Republics had been on the cards for a considerable time before the war finally broke out in September 1899. Discussions had been going on for years between Britain and the Boers about the relationship of the Boer states to their neighbouring British colonies. Things finally came to a head in May 1899 when a conference was held in Bloemfontein in an attempt to resolve the most recent points of contention. It proved to be the last chance of preventing a war. Kruger, President of the Transvaal, represented the Boers; Sir Alfred Milner, High Commissioner in the Cape, led the British delegation. It was held in the capital of the second Boer Republic, the Orange Free State, but the Free State President, Marthinus Steyn, did not take part. Steyn and his government had been supporting Kruger in his stand against British interference in Boer affairs, but they were far less belligerent than the Transvaalers and did not want war. The meeting had been set up on Steyn's instigation. Milner agreed to meet Kruger but insisted that Steyn should not take part in the discussions.

The main argument between the British government and the Transvaal was about the rights of 'Uitlanders' (foreigners) on the Transvaal goldfields. The gold rush had attracted thousands of people into the Transvaal; many came from Europe and even America and Australia, but most were British citizens. By the 1890s these Uitlanders were paying a considerable amount of tax and were vociferously demanding equal rights. The central question was the period of residence before they could get the right to vote in Transvaal elections. Kruger had been insisting on fifteen years, but he had come to Bloemfontein to agree on a compromise. Milner, one of a breed of new British imperialists, demanded immediate voting rights for all Uitlanders who had lived for more than five years in the Transvaal. Those who qualified already outnumbered the Transvaal burghers. The old man burst into a tearful 'It is our country you want'. Milner abruptly terminated the meeting without consulting Joseph Chamberlain (then Secretary of State for the Colonies in Lord Salisbury's Unionist government), who had already cabled him to continue negotiating. The instruction arrived too late to stop Milner pushing the Boers into a war which he clearly wanted. How had this impasse come about?

The differences between Britain and the Republics were much more deep-seated than an argument about voting rights. To get a clear understanding of the problem, one has to go back to the earliest days of their relationship. Within a short time of Britain taking over the Cape, the English- and Dutch-speaking elements of the population were at loggerheads. The southern tip of Africa was first used as a re-victualling station for Dutch East Indian ships on the way to India. It was not envisaged as a permanent colony. But the religious wars in Europe led many Protestants to look for safety in distant lands and the Cape of Good Hope seemed to have much to offer. The first true colonists came mainly from Holland. Although they were joined by French Huguenots and Germans, Dutch remained the official language. It was not long before the colonists began to resent the authoritarianism of the Dutch East India Company which ran the colony.

During the Napoleonic Wars British troops occupied the Cape because of its strategic importance. Later the British government bought the territory from Holland. The colonists were thus transferred to British rule with no consultation. At first they welcomed the change, but the British authorities began introducing laws which seemed clearly to be aimed at destroying the sense of identity that the colonists had already developed. Their grievances mounted rapidly as more and more 'anti-Dutch' laws were brought in: burgher councils were abolished, the Dutch legal system was swept aside and an attempt was made to deny them the use of the Dutch language in the law courts. The colonists were further infuriated by changes in the system of land tenure and by the liberty given to black people. The freeing of slaves in 1834 caused particular anger; the colonists' system of farming depended on slaves, who were seen as part of a man's property. The British government offered compensation for the slaves, but it had to be collected in England. Most colonists were forced to employ financial agents in England to get their money and the charges of these middle-men were often exorbitant. These changes relating to the black people of the Cape were introduced with a singular lack of understanding by the authorities. The colonists had a seventeenth-century attitude to race. If the changes had been introduced with subtlety it is likely that there would have been little opposition; as it was they not only resulted in a great deal of bitterness, but soured the colonists' relationship with the blacks in the colony and set the pattern for their attitude to the black tribes they encountered when they left the Cape.

For a time the Kaffir War of 1834 diverted the Dutch colonists' attention from their grievances. The blacks were pushed back beyond the Kei river in the eastern Cape, leaving an empty territory which the colonists wanted. They had taken part in the fighting alongside British and Hottentot troops and hoped that the authorities in Cape Town would allow them to farm this distant area, and that there they would be able to continue a Dutch style of life. However, this idea was blocked by the administration and the area was annexed by the Cape Colony. Apparently thwarted at every turn by their British oppressors, the colonists began looking towards the vast interior of the continent, previously only visited by hunters and adventurers, to set up an independent state. After careful organization, groups of families set out in columns of ox-wagons which slowly 'trekked' inland. Within a couple of years nearly half the non-British population had left the Cape. The word 'Boer' means farmer; *trekboers* in the Dutch colony were farmers looking for new farms. The whole migration became known as the 'Great Trek'. Dutch colonists who remained in the Cape came to be called 'Afrikanders'. In this book the term Afrikanders will be used in this way. It should not be confused with the more modern word 'Afrikaners', which only came into wide use after the Boer War as a unifying term to describe all white people in South Africa who spoke the new language Afrikaans.

The trek forged what the British saw as a group of malcontents into a unified nation – the Boers. It had elements of a biblical saga. Although the trekkers did not have to face extreme conditions (they were never far from water and the country was full of wild animals which could be shot for food), they did suffer severe hardships. Many died from illness; others were killed during encounters with hostile black tribes. They began to see themselves as members of a chosen race like the Israelites of the Old Testament; and like the Israelites they looked forward to their Promised Land.

To the Victorian Englishman the trekkers were primitives who had run away from civilization, while the Boers saw the trek primarily as giving freedom from British oppression. Unfortunately for them this did not last long: Britain was soon meddling in their affairs. A group of Boers settled near Durban and declared the region an independent republic. Britain could not afford to lose an important deep-water harbour on the way to India, so troops were dispatched to secure the area and in 1845 Natal became a British colony. Britain justified the act by asserting that all Boers still owed allegiance to the Crown, since there were no well-defined boundaries between the Cape and the interior. The Boers were too weak to resist and trekked back inland.

For the remainder of the nineteenth century the concept that Britain had sovereignty over the whole of the southern part of the continent remained the main point of contention between the two sides. It came up again and again in their relationship. Even when the Boers did manage to set up two self-governing states, Britain held the right to interfere, if imperial interests deemed it necessary. But for the moment the Boers were left alone. The interior seemed dangerous and barren, and the land in the Cape satisfied the needs of the British colonists.

The two Boer 'Republics' lay on the high flatlands called the 'veld'. The Boers called the country between the Orange and the Vaal Rivers the 'Orange River Territory'; to the north lay the 'Transvaal'. In 1852, at a convention held at Sand River, Britain granted the Transvaal rights of self-government. Two years later they gave similar rights to the 'Orange River Sovereignty'. Thus, with the two British colonies of the Cape and Natal, there were now four separate states in southern Africa at varying stages of self-government. The Boer states could possibly have separated themselves completely from British control because there seemed to be little of interest for Britain in the veld. However, the Orange Free State maintained close connections with the Cape, and the Transvaal needed British help from time to time because of political and financial difficulties.

In 1867 diamonds were unexpectedly found near the Orange River. Within months the find attracted fortune hunters from all over the world, many of them British. The first railways were begun. By 1871 a dispute had arisen over the ownership of the area. Apart from the Orange Free State, a number of black and coloured contenders laid claims to the area of the diamond fields. The Free State asked the British to settle the matter, and Natal's Lieutenant-Governor was appointed as an independent arbitrator. He decided in favour of a coloured man, Nicholas Waterboer, who was leader of the local Griqua tribe. The Free State government accepted the decision, but were incensed when the Griqua territory was annexed by the Cape shortly afterwards and the diamond fields fell into British hands. The town of Kimberley grew up next to the biggest mine and the whole industry became dominated by Cecil Rhodes.

In 1877 the Transvaal got into difficulty. The state was nearly bankrupt and black tribes threatened on all sides. Help was sought from Britain, particularly by British residents in the Transvaal. The current British Secretary of State for the Colonies, Lord Carnarvon, had for some time been hoping to unite the whole of South Africa in a federation of states. He sent a representative, Sir Theophilus Shepstone, to the Transvaal to settle the difficulty by annexation. Dutch-speaking colonists in the Cape as well as those in the Free State and the Transvaal protested, but took no immediate action. However, it was not long before the Transvaalers demanded self-government again. There was a delay in settling the issue, caused by the Zulu king, Cetewayo, who slaughtered a column of British troops at Isandhlwana in Zululand and was not defeated until July 1879. The following year Boer anger at the annexation was again diverted by an uprising of the Basuto tribe which had to be settled by British troops. After the blacks had been defeated, the Boers took affairs into their own hands and revolted. The campaign of 1881 between the Transvaal and Britain is known in South Africa as the First Boer War of Independence. The fighting was at first characterized by the siege of British outposts and by small engagements. A larger British column was then dispatched from Natal. The Boer commandos attacked and defeated it at Majuba Hill, killing its commander, General Colley. These commandos were led by Piet Joubert, who was to became the first Commandant-General in the Boer War of this book. Gladstone was Prime Minister at the time, and he soon made peace with the Boers. His rapid settlement, which was opposed by many British politicians, left the Boers with the idea that the Liberal Party could be counted on to support them. In Britain today few people know about this first Boer War, but it has left the erroneous impression that British troops in the 1899 Boer War still wore red uniforms in battle.

In 1886 it was the turn of the Transvaal to find unexpected riches. Gold was discovered on an area known as the Witwatersrand only 30 miles from Pretoria. The gold rush attracted thousands of foreigners, mostly from Britain. These were the Uitlanders who were to become so central to the debate at the Bloemfontein conference. Within a few months the town of Johannesburg sprang up. It is still growing, on wealth from the richest reef of gold ever discovered. In 1883 Kruger was elected President of the Transvaal, in which this mining-camp (unwanted by many Transvaal burghers) had sprung up. Shortly afterwards he visited London and attended a convention to define the borders of the Transvaal. He met Gladstone and other statesmen, and then travelled to Holland and Germany. It was an important landmark for the Boers: not only had their affairs received sympathetic public attention but Kruger had showed himself able to meet world diplomats on their own level and thus enhanced his prestige.

However, political problems were growing at home. Many of the Transvaal's difficulties were with the local blacks, but problems from the goldfields gradually began to dominate the political scene. Rhodes now had extensive business interests in the Johannesburg goldfields. In 1889 the British government granted his 'South African Company' a charter to administer and develop the large territory on the Transvaal's northern border. The area was then occupied by Rhodes's private army, led by his protégé Dr Leander Starr Jameson. The charter was an important coup for Rhodes and helped him to be elected Prime Minister of the Cape. The region, named Rhodesia, was administered by Jameson. In 1894 the Company's army took over the area around Mafeking on the Transvaal's western border. This was partly to prevent a Transvaal invasion, which had been threatened. Rhodes was now in a curious position: as Cape Prime Minister he was having to maintain good relations with Kruger, while at the same time being directly, if surreptitiously, involved in a border dispute with his republic.

Kruger now began to obstruct British interests in the Transvaal. He prevented the Transvaal from entering a customs union with the Cape, and refused transport wagons containing British mining equipment free access to the Reef mines. Meanwhile a committee of Reformers was set up by Uitlanders in Johannesburg. They began demanding the same rights of representation as the burghers, and asked for improvements in municipal services and schools. They were particularly angry about the 'concessions' which Kruger had been handing out to Dutchmen and Germans in Pretoria, giving them monopolies on importing goods or making equipment for the mines. This practice naturally encouraged corruption.

In 1893 Kruger was elected for the second time, by a narrow majority over Joubert, who led a party which wanted conciliation with the Uitlanders. The result was so close that it had to be 'validated' by a 'committee of investigation'. The Reformers then appealed to the British government for help, while Rhodes decided to support them in open revolt. Reformers prepared secret stores of weapons in Johannesburg and Jameson was instructed to prepare a mounted invasion force in Mafeking which could ride into the Transvaal if trouble broke out.

In December 1895 the world was electrified by news that Jameson had marched into the Transvaal with 800 Company 'volunteers'. Jameson's excuse for the invasion, an undated written plea for help from the Uitlander leaders, was fraudulent. Rhodes had not authorized the action and telegraphed him at once to stop; it was one thing to intervene after a spontaneous rebellion, quite another to do so before any outbreak had occurred. But the wire had been cut and the message never arrived. The Reformers made a feeble attempt to set up a provisional government and then fell over themselves to surrender. Jameson and his men were captured ignominiously by the first Boer commando they met. Even Kruger was surprised at the ease with which the rebellion was put down. The leaders were tried and convicted of treason. Some were sentenced to death, though later they were released after paying heavy fines. There is considerable evidence that Joseph Chamberlain knew of Rhodes's plans beforehand, but at the time he was not seen to be implicated. Rhodes, who at once resigned the Cape premiership, took all the blame when he returned to England for the enquiry. He was publicly discredited and forced to relinquish his position in the Chartered Company.

Kruger's status was enormously strengthened both at home and abroad (there was even a telegram of support from the Kaiser), and in 1898 he was re-elected with an overwhelming majority. The same year Sir Alfred Milner took over as British Representative in the Cape. He had openly declared his opposition to the regime in Pretoria and particularly to 'Krugerism'. The Transvaal government responded to British criticism by trying to improve the administration, but their efforts did not satisfy Milner. He received a petition of complaint from the Uitlanders after an Englishman had been shot during an arrest, and the seriousness of the position began to claim world attention in increasingly large headlines. After an extensive exchange of correspondence and numerous diplomatic manoeuvres, Kruger and Milner met in Bloemfontein for the conference of May 1899.

After the conference Kruger made a number of changes in Transvaal law. Franchise was offered to Uitlanders who had been resident for more than nine years; more representation was given to residents in the goldfields. These and other concessions were pressed on him by Afrikander politicians in the Cape, who hoped that they would satisfy the demands of the British government and particularly of Milner. They did not, however, meet with a positive response from the British side. Telegrams flashed between the various parties, Milner replying to all proposals of arbitration that he could not recommend further discussions until all the Uitlanders' grievances had been settled. As the situation worsened a document was drawn up by Kruger's cabinet, asking for further arbitration. Whitehall began hurriedly dispatching army reinforcements to Africa. Kruger in turn insisted that their movement towards the Transvaal border should be stopped. An ultimatum was drawn up by Jan Smuts, a brilliant Cape lawyer who had moved to the Transvaal to help the Boers and had joined Kruger's government. It demanded that British troops on the Transvaal's borders be withdrawn and reinforcements on the way sent back. It is a measure of the division of opinion in the Boer camp that this ultimatum was not dispatched for more than a week. The last days were spent trying to ensure that the Orange Free State would honour the treaty to support the Transvaal if war broke out. 'The day I say war,' was Steyn's reply, 'it will be war to the bitter end.' It is a phrase which still reverberates in South Africa.

Kruger did not have things all his own way. Even in the Transvaal parliament he had trouble. He was opposed by a group led by 'Koos' de la Rey and Louis Botha, who were later to became the best Transvaal commandants. De la Rey insisted that the Boers would need at least ten years' preparation to win a war against a European power. After a final jibe from Kruger that he was a coward, he rose and replied that he would do his duty: 'You will see me in the field fighting for your independence long after you and your party who make war with your mouths have fled the country.'

By 9 October all hope of peace had faded. Even Steyn consented to the Transvaal's ultimatum being sent. The British Cabinet replied that its nature was such that Her Majesty's Government found it 'impossible to discuss'. They were at war. The Great Trek had created the Boer nation; the war was about to destroy it.

2. THE TWO ARMIES

THE BRITISH ARMY

In 1899 the British army was thought to be in peak condition. It was, however, designed to defend small uprisings all over an empire, not to fight a major war. Campaigns which had been fought since the Crimea had not needed the mobilization of large numbers of troops for any one region; instead small garrisons were established in most British territories. But because of financial constraints, changes in the distribution of its garrisons in the last quarter of the century had left South Africa, which at the time posed no military threat, without a large enough force to defeat the Boer attack. During the negotiations of 1899 the South African garrison was not reinforced because the British government did

9. General Campbell with orderly.

not want to be provocative. The nearest large force was in India, where there were 150,000 seasoned native troops, but these were never used against the Boers, being regarded as essential to peace-keeping on the troubled northern frontier. It was decided also to restrict the fighting to white men. A second Indian mutiny was still a possibility and it is likely that the High Command worried that Indian troops might get a taste for defeating white armies.

The British government was very concerned about its military weakness in South Africa, but it was hoped that a few weeks would see a great difference. Once sufficient troops could be brought into the country, no great difficulty was envisaged in defeating a Boer attack. The British army considered itself to be more than a match for a rabble of farmers: more than thirty successful campaigns had been carried out against a variety of 'native' uprisings in the Empire and in Egypt. Senior officers had wide experience of military administration; the army was well fed, well clothed and backed up by a modern transport system. Khaki uniforms had been used for years and most regiments had considerable tropical experience. The young officers, especially those who had campaigned in India, had a healthy scepticism of Aldershot training. Morale was high.

British equipment was modern. The Lee-Enfield Mk I rifle, introduced in 1895, and the Lee-Metfords, although not quite as good as the Boer Mausers, were fine weapons. The artillery was

10. Indian troops in Cape Town.

a great source of pride: field guns and howitzers had been tested under a great variety of battle conditions; most units had Maxim guns (later called machine guns). In the first battles they did not have the Maxim-Nordenfeldt automatic cannon, called the 'pom-pom', which was a disadvantage, but British shells for the larger guns were loaded with lyddite, a high explosive said to kill everything within fifty yards by its detonation, and over a much wider area with its poisonous fumes. Nevertheless, major deficiencies soon became evident. There was a marked distinction between the Indian army and the home command, and the two seldom met. Officers on both sides looked down on each other: the home command considered itself to be socially superior, while the Indian Army was proud of its practical experience. Older officers in Britain were dominated by a parade-ground theory of war. They were more interested in moving cavalry elegantly and positioning artillery correctly than in infantry tactics. The biggest deficiency

11. The 'thin khaki line'. Before the Boer War British troops were trained to shoot in volley. Here the middle rank is ready to fire. As soon as they have done so, they step back to reload and the kneeling line stands up to take their places. Meanwhile the rear line moves forward into the kneeling position.

was in infantry training. Only cavalry troops were taught to ride, although both armies in the American Civil War, and later Roosevelt's army in the Cuban campaign, had proved the value of mounted infantry. In the first weeks of the war offers of mounted infantry from the colonies were turned down.

In addition the conditions of army service were still oldfashioned. Men signed on for at least six years, after which it was very difficult to begin another career. Low pay discouraged the idea of army service for ambitious men, and it was virtually impossible to rise from the ranks. It was a standing joke that regular soldiers received much less pay than volunteers ('the one shilling and thrupences helping the five bobs again'). The men were unhealthy and ill-educated. Officers were taught to use them as 'machines of war': great stress was laid on keeping them 'well in hand', 'standing them up to fire' and allowing them only to shoot in volley. There was little or no training in marksmanship, and camouflage was not considered sportsmanlike. Autonomous action in battle was strictly discouraged.

12. 'The Worcesters leading the attack.'

Most officers looked upon war as an extension of their activities on the cricket or polo field, combined with the excitement of a grouse shoot. Newspaper articles and private letters are filled with sporting terms. Artillery 'pitched its shells well up'; a column sent to capture Boers was called a 'drive'; a line of troops ordered to advance with full equipment into the fire of Mauser rifles were called 'beaters'. Today it is difficult for Britons to understand how their grandfathers were prepared to walk slowly into a 'valley of death' as they did in the Boer War and the Great War:

Our indomitable men walked erect and straight onward. Not Rome in her palmiest days ever possessed more devout sons. As the gladiators marched proud and becoming to meet death, so the British soldiers doomed to die saluted, and then with alacrity stepped forward to do their duty and win a glorious grave. There never was a better infantry than ours; each individual linesman is a far grander hero than ninety-nine hundredths of the people in England have any conception of. Rough he may be, but the stuff that makes for Empires and for greatness fills every vein and heart-beat. Anglo-Saxon soldiers always advance in this way.

Stirring stuff, but the writer added:

Perhaps there may be occasions when the sight of men coming on so steadily in the face of almost certain death will try the nerves of their antagonists, but my view is that, save where men have to get within running distance of a few lines of trenches, the system of rushes from cover to cover by small squads is far less wasteful of life.[1]

Of course it was not like that at all. A lieutenant of the King's Royal Rifles wrote home after the battle of Dundee:

When we got the order to advance my heart was rather in my mouth, as I knew we were under fire, and in a minute or two I might be a corpse or rather cold. However up I had to get and give my men a lead. They all behaved splendidly. Bullets came whizzing past unpleasantly. I was dying to run to get to the wood. However, I got so excited I forgot everything.
Half-way across the open was a fence and getting over there some poor fellows were shot; at least we got to the fence ... In the wood there were plenty of ditches, and at the end of the wood was a wall. We lay there to get breath. Poor Hambro was shot through the jaw, but would take no notice. Then came the bad part. There was a bramble hedge on the top of the wall, so one could not get over, but there was a gateway, and through this we had to go, and it was a hot time. But there were some beautiful rocks about fifty yards off, so not much damage was done ... When I got about half-way up the hill I found myself next to Hambro, who had been wounded twice; we lay down under the rocks, as the firing was very heavy. We saw lots of men shot as they crossed the wall. Hambro and I had to retire. I had my helmet knocked off with a piece of rock the shell hit. When I went up the hill a second time, Hambro was lying almost dead, with his legs reduced to pulp. Too terrible! I suppose a shell must have hit him behind. We must have been there for an hour, bullets whizzing over us. Colonel Sherston was dying; his groans were awful.

Then an awful part happened – our artillery, mistaking us for Boers, began firing on us. Colonel Gunning, who was just below me, stood up and yelled out, 'Stop that firing!' These were the last words I heard him speak, but I believe his last words were, 'Remember you are Riflemen.'[2]

Technical developments could have been used more effectively. There was no radio, but the army had an excellent field telegraph system. The electric telegraph had been developed before the Crimean War, and although it could easily be interrupted by cutting the wire, it proved invaluable. At the begining, however, most officers relied on the heliograph, a method of signalling with mirror-directed sunlight, which depended on the weather and could be seen by the Boers. Transport was a problem in the veld. Steam engines were tried but were of little use when operating far from a water supply. The army even brought out to South Africa a number of hydrogen-filled balloons for reconnaissance, but their full potential was not realized. For instance, observers could have been trained as photographers and used cameras with telephoto lenses.

13 (*below*). Signalling with a heliograph.

14 (*top right*). Military steam engine. The army took a number of steam engines to South Africa, but they proved to be of limited value because of the lack of water in the veld.

15 (*bottom right*). A rare sight in South Africa during the Boer War: a petrol-driven motor car. Away from the railway lines the British army had to rely on horses, mule-carts and ox-wagons for transport.

16 (*left*). Print of a glass-plate negative from the Boer War collection of Durban Museum, where its significance as one of the earliest aerial photographs was not appreciated. No other such photograph has so far come to light despite a careful search through collections of Boer War photographs in South Africa and Britain. It has been examined by Captain H.B. Eaton (ret.) of the RAF reconnaissance unit, JARIC. He agrees that it appears to be a genuine aerial photograph, probably taken from a balloon at about 1,000 feet. It shows a military camp containing most of an infantry battalion, a possible cavalry or mounted infantry regiment and a headquarters or administrative unit.

17 (*inset*). Observation balloon on the march. The Royal Engineers took three hydrogen-balloon detatchments to South Africa in 1899.

There is an interesting sidelight on the balloons. The Boers knew a great deal about them – even President Kruger had gone up in one when visiting France. Amongst the back-velders, however, they caused some excitement and even fear. It was a source of considerable amusement in the British press when the Boers reported that Britain was using them to fly over the countryside and might even bomb cities from them. They were of course anchored with ropes. But there still remains a mystery. On 24 October 1899 an official telegram was received at Boer Headquarters: 'Balloons – Yesterday evening two balloons were seen at Irene, proceeding in the direction of Springs. Official telegraphists instructed to inform the Commander-in-Chief about any objects seen in the sky.'[3] On the same day numerous 'balloons' were seen all over the place, travelling in all sorts of directions. The official telegrams contain a number of such reports. In the early evening powerful 'searchlights' were seen moving about the sky. All telegraph officers were instructed to notify the authorities immediately

18. Young city Boers.

19. The Transvaal State Artillery in 1899 with Major Albrecht (left, with beard) in command.

one was sighted. Everyone seems to have been watching the sky and the sightings are usually considered to be the result of Boer hysteria. Today, in an age well used to UFOs, they would be given another interpretation.

THE BOER ARMY

Whatever the British thought of the Boer army, the Boers themselves had every reason to be satisfied with it. It had been carefully designed for the conditions of the South African veld. The Boers had an efficient mechanism for mobilizing their army which had its origin in the way men were sent on commando to defend the convoys during the Great Trek. Each state elected a Commandant-General. In 1899 the Transvaal had Piet Joubert, who had led the Boers in 1881. He was appointed Commander-in-Chief of both republican forces. Neither the Transvaal nor the Orange Free State possessed a standing army or a general

20. Father and son going on commando. Notice their small Boer ponies. The photograph was taken with an old camera which did not have an achromatic lens.

staff. The only professional units were the state artilleries. Although small, they were equipped with the most modern guns, and even had field telegraphs. The Transvaal unit was commanded by a Boer; the Free State's senior officer was a German soldier, Major Albrecht, who had been brought into the country to bring the Boers up to date in modern gunnery. Training was so good that the British were as surprised by their gunmanship as by the speed with which they moved into inaccessible positions. The Transvaal had another small professional unit for defence, the South African Police (known as the 'Zarps'). But their real military strength lay in having a citizen army: all able-bodied burghers between 16 and 60 had to be available for military service.

During an emergency burghers were ordered to prepare for military duty, known as 'going on commando'. Each man was

21. Group photograph of a small commando with Commandant Bosman (hands in pockets). Notice the lack of uniforms.

expected to provide himself with a horse, rifle, ammunition and sufficient food to last for eight days. Traditional campaign rations consisted of biscuits and dried meat called 'biltong'. If hostilities lasted longer than eight days it became the government's responsibility to feed and arm the men. Burghers expected to go on commando from time to time and were well prepared: they kept their rifles at home.

Some burghers were exempt from commando service. These included members of the Volksraad, state officials, ministers of the Church, teachers, dealers (whatever that meant) and the only sons of widows. Others could be excused from duty if they found sufficient 'lawful and well-founded reasons' to satisfy the local commandant. The system was decentralized. Each region had its own commando which could be mobilized more rapidly than many a permanent army. These varied in size from 300 to 3,000 men, depending on the local population, and each made its own transport arrangements. At the beginning the commandos were the fighting units, but later in the war they were often broken into smaller tactical groups. Within the forty administrative regions, commandants were elected for five years. They in turn appointed one or two junior officers, called 'Veld-Cornets', who had the power to 'commandeer' anything the commando required. It was

22. A *kriegsraad*, or pre-battle tactical meeting. The photograph shows Commandant Botha's *kriegsgraad* before the Battle of Colenso (December 1899).

23. Electing a Veld-Cornet.

possible for the government to call up foreign residents for commando duty (and a few British residents did volunteer), but the majority who remained in the Republics during the war were not called up. Often, however, supplies were commandeered from them.

The Boer army was remarkable in many ways. Although burghers were legally obliged to take up arms when ordered, the government did not have the right to demand unconditional obedience. Authority was imposed by reasoned argument or persuasion. Even battle discipline depended on voluntary cooperation. If a man did not want to fight in a particular battle, he could (and often did) ask for leave. It was laid down that not more than 10 per cent of a commando could be away at any one time, but the rule was not strictly applied in the early battles. The idiosyncrasy of this army is most clearly demonstrated in the way it prepared for battle. A meeting of the commandants known as a *kriegsraad* was called. It was chaired by the most senior officer of the region in which the battle was to take place. The coming engagement was discussed and various tactics proposed. All commandants, whatever their seniority, had the right to make suggestions. Finally a policy was

agreed by consensus. Commandants would then return to their commandos and explain what had been decided. Rarely, a commandant would disagree with the plan and advise his men not to take part in the coming battle, or sometimes the burghers themselves would decide that the tactics were poor and would refuse to fight. In some of the major battles, British troops saw armed burghers watching from suitable vantage points, some even accompanied by their wives. In spite of these remarkably military practices, the Boers were excellent fighters. If a man took part in a battle he did so with a thorough understanding of what was required and could be relied on to do his duty.

Another factor which welded the Boers into an efficient fighting force was the highly organized structure of their society. This is best illustrated by contrasting them with fictional film cowboys, who look so similar to the modern eye. The Boers too had crossed a continent in wagons, worked huge cattle farms in a 'Western' landscape, were constantly in the saddle and carried guns. But the similarities end there. Theirs was not a society of individualists. They saw themselves (and still do) as members of a God-chosen

24. Boers watching the fight at Dundee.

race with close social and family ties holding them united against foreign enemies. Leaders were God-appointed; they trusted in Him for victory. Alcohol was forbidden; the image of the maverick was not venerated; age, experience and leadership were greatly respected. Today, men who fought for the Boer Republics are hero-figures to the Afrikaans nation. It was different at the time. The relationship between the men and their leaders was one of respect, tempered with a teasing familiarity. Even when discipline was tightened, camaraderie between officers and men remained close. De Wet and Botha often slept in the same tent as private burghers. There were no official badges of office or medals. It was a true citizens' army.

They fought as a team, not waiting for an official order to take advantage of an opportunity or to retreat when a position became untenable. Until the development of the highly trained professional soldier of today, no army had had such good marksmen. For fifty years they had relied on their own weapons, although their early muzzle-loaders had been notoriously inaccurate. They were trained to save ammunition, which was expensive and difficult to obtain in the veld, and their accuracy with the new German Mauser rifles was phenomenal. Although American gun experts said that it was impossible to aim accurately beyond 800 yards, there is overwhelming evidence that the Boers could pick off British officers at 1,200 yards and sometimes further.

The British official history of the war estimates the entire Boer army at just over 87,000 men. Boer sources say that the figure was nearer 60,000. They had no reserves. At the end of the war there were still more than 27,000 men in the commandos, although about 4,000 had been killed and 26,000 were held in prison camps. It required more than 400,000 British troops to win, and even then neither republican army was defeated outright. Boer tactics were designed to prevent casualties. Commandants preferred an ambush to other methods of attack. They liked to fight on ground which had previously been carefully studied and marked for distance – De Wet even fought one engagement on his own farm. They disliked hand-to-hand fighting: the traditional mode of attack was to lie in wait on a suitable koppie where they could hide behind large stones. When the shooting started (heralded by a signal shot from the commandant), their smokeless powder did not give away their location. If their position were threatened they would run to their ponies behind the hill and would soon be out of range. However, during the course of the war these tactics underwent considerable change.

At the start of the war the Boers were in a strong position. It is possible that they could have achieved outright victory in the first few months if they had devoted as much attention to strategy as they did to tactical superiority. They had a numerical advantage and greater mobility. The commandos were faster than the British units. Each man had at least one small, strong African pony, bred to withstand the harsh conditions of the veld.

The Boers were also better armed than the British. After the Jameson raid Kruger had spent a fortune on weapons, many of which were of British manufacture. Martini-Henry and Lee-Metford rifles were bought in England and imported through Portuguese East Africa in English ships. Some were even landed in Cape Town. Twelve million rounds of rifle ammunition were purchased through Beckett and Company of Pretoria, the Transvaal agents of Kynoch's of Birmingham. Some of the Boer pom-poms, or Maxim-Nordenfeldt guns, bore inscriptions showing that they had been made in London. Some of the the equipment which passed through British territory was labelled as agricultural machinery. (Perhaps this is the origin of the story which appeared in newspapers during the Falklands war, that South Africa was shipping arms to the Argentine in crates labelled as agricultural equipment.) The Boers' basic infantry weapon was the new German Mauser 303 rifle. Krupp cannons, also from Germany, proved to

25 (*below*). General Cronje (with whip) and his men manning one of the large 'Long Tom' siege-guns at Mafeking.

26 (*below right*). Boer 'pom-pom'.

27 (*overleaf*). A group of Boer photographs showing Boers just called out on commando. Note their old clothes and modern weapons.

be the best field-guns of the war and more than a match for the older weapons used by the British artillery. The Boers also had a number of large siege-guns, made by Creusot in France and known as 'Long Toms', which could out-distance any of the British guns. These were used to shell the besieged towns. By 1889 the strength of the Transvaal artillery had been increased to more than a thousand men. The Boers might have had an overwhelming superiority of weapons if Joubert, who opposed a war, had not done his utmost to prevent the Transvaal government from ordering as many guns as Kruger wanted. Delays caused in this way meant that more than 70 artillery pieces were prevented from landing in Lourenço Marques by the British navy, which blockaded the port as soon as the war started.

It was the spirit of the men which lay at the core of Boer strength; it was their arrogance which let them down. They considered themselves to be better fighters than any Englishman; they were better armed and better prepared to withstand a South African war than the British soldier; they were confident that they would 'push the troops into the sea'.

FOREIGN VOLUNTEERS

The Boers were offered considerable help from Europe. This came not from European governments but from ordinary citizens amongst whom the Boer cause was popular. The idea of two little states facing the might of the British Empire seems to have been too much for many a republican. University students in Europe took up the Boer cause with particular enthusiasm. In a manner reminiscent of the Spanish Civil War, thousands of people from all walks of life tried to volunteer, though few managed to get to South Africa. The Boers themselves made no attempt to recruit outsiders and regarded the volunteers as a mixed blessing. They were welcomed as a token of possible future official assistance by their respective governments but also resented by Boers who felt that they were quite able to fight their own battle. In Europe everything was done to discourage people from joining. Many governments made strong pro-Boer comments, but neither France nor Germany, who could have helped, was prepared to face the British Empire. Later in the war France and Russia tried to get a European initiative going to help the Boers, but they were blocked by Germany.

The European volunteers joined local foreigners to form national units in a 'foreign brigade' of about 1,600 men. Among them were Irish, Americans, Germans, Scandinavians, French, Dutch and Russians. Although an insignificant addition to the Boer army, they gave the fight an international flavour. They formed a very mixed and interesting bunch of people. There were many members of the European military aristocracy, such as De Gelder of the Dutch cavalry, Comte Villebois-Mareuil from the French Foreign Legion, the German Count Sternberg and Prince Bagration of Tiflis, who brought two Cossack servants. These were mostly demonstrating their anti-British feeling. The mass of European volunteers offered their services for a variety of reasons. The majority were simple people who felt that Britain was treating the Boers unfairly. Some were adventurers; others were secret military observers. The number also included a few Britons who, having settled in the country, felt allegiance to their new home. There were even some American miners from the Transvaal. Many of the Europeans spent all their money getting to Africa and were penniless when they were returned home. Most of them finally became disillusioned with the indifference of the Boers, who had great difficulty in understanding their motives. To them the fight was not for republicanism against imperialism, but for freedom from English tyranny.

Foreigners often distinguished themselves in battle. On occasion they suffered a much higher casualty rate than the Boers alongside

whom they fought. This was true of the Germans under Colonel Schiel at Elandslaagte, and of the Hollander corps in Natal. At Magersfontein, a platoon of the Scandinavian Corps was nearly wiped out. They had been set to guard the Boer flank and were overrun by Highlanders when they moved on to open ground to cut off the retreating Scotsmen. Only seven of the fifty-three escaped; thirty-nine were killed. The president of the Transvaal Scandinavian Organization afterwards reported that the body of their leader, Field-Cornet Flygare, and that of Baron Fagerskold had been stripped and robbed.

If one had to single out a few examples of those foreigners who were most useful to the Boers, they would have to be Roger Albrecht, who organized and trained the Free State Artillery and was captured at Paardeberg with Cronje, Colonel John Blake, leader of the Irish contingent, and Comte George Villebois-Mareuil, who eventually led the foreign brigade. The latter was a quixotic figure, much loved by the Boers. He frequently com-

28. President Botha welcoming American volunteers.

29. Georges de Villebois-Mareuil, commander of the Foreign Brigade in the Boer army.

plained that, although they listened to him courteously, they always rejected his professional advice. After the battle of Paardeberg he reorganized all the foreigners into a single commando and became the first foreign *vecht-general*. He died tragically and unnecessarily at Boshof in the Free State early in April 1900, attacking a force commanded by Lord Methuen. Despite a warning that the British column occupying the region consisted of 7,000 men rather than the 500 he had anticipated, he attacked with a small force. The Boers considered that his rash decision to make a stand against overwhelming odds resulted from excess sun during his long ride before the battle.

The case of the Irish is of special interest. It must be remembered that a considerable part of the British army consisted of Irish regiments. The situation was similar to that of the American War of Independence, in which Irishmen formed a significant part of the British army, while a number of Washington's men were Irish volunteers. In that war they played a crucial role in staying

with the American general through the harsh winter at Valley Forge when things were going badly for him. The majority of those Irish who joined the Boers were republicans, some of whom later returned to Ireland and took part in the Easter Rising of 1916.

Before the war, Irish Members of Parliament had spoken strongly against the South African policies of Chamberlain and Milner, and the mood amongst the nationalist parties in Ireland was strongly pro-Boer. When war became inevitable, several hundred men volunteered to fight against the British. In South Africa they joined an Irish Brigade which had been formed by Transvaal residents. The idea of a separate Irish unit is credited to John MacBride, leader of the South African Irish nationalist community, who had been active in the Fenian movement in Dublin, and after moving to South Africa in 1896 had built up considerable political influence among Irish workers on the Rand. The proposal was made at a meeting of the Johannesburg '98 Centenary Committee on 3 October 1899. It was decided to send a deputation to Kruger to ask for full citizenship for volunteers. Kruger agreed to the request, but refused to allow them to campaign in Ireland and America for more volunteers. Always suspicious of the motives of foreigners who wanted to fight for the Boer cause, he told one such group: 'Thank you for coming. Don't imagine that we have need of you. The Transvaal wants no foreign help but if you wish to fight for us you are welcome.'

Another meeting was called, and the First Irish Brigade was officially constituted. MacBride was nominated as commander, but he felt that his lack of military training made him unsuitable. Instead the appointment was given to Colonel J.Y.F Blake, an American of Irish ancestry living in Johannesburg. He had been trained at West Point and had served in the United States Cavalry, getting campaign experience in the Apache wars in Arizona. In a fit of enthusiasm a manifesto was issued calling on other Irishmen in South Africa to join and ending, as might be expected, on a note of Irish rather than Boer patriotism.

Not all the Brigade were Irish; there were Americans from the Rand mines and at least ten Frenchmen among the original members. Although never more than 200 strong, they did good work for the Boers. Early in October they travelled to Pretoria just in time to take part in Joubert's invasion of Natal. The Brigade formed part of the attacking force at Dundee, but the majority of its members did little fighting during the remainder of the year while they were attached to the commandos investing Ladysmith, though some were sent to the Tugela line, and took part in battles at Colenso and Spionkop. A few were killed at the battle of Pepworth Hill at the start of the Ladysmith investment in October, when Blake was wounded. When he returned to the siege after

30. Major J. MacBride in his Boer War dress, holding the sight of a captured British gun.

convalescing, he is said to have spent his time (perhaps more constructively than most) trying to work out a scheme for using kites to drop bombs on the town. Joubert, however, disapproved.

In February 1900 a group of fifty Americans arrived to join the Boers. They had been organized by Irish societies in Massachusetts and Chicago. To get official recognition from the American Red Cross, they had signed affidavits saying that they were going to serve as non-combatants, but although there were four doctors in the unit, the majority intended to take part in the fighting. They were unlucky enough to arrive just in time to join the Brigade as it retreated in front of Roberts's massive advance. As soon as things got really bad some of the men left for home, but the majority remained in Africa until late in 1900. The last action in which they fought as a unit was during an unsuccessful Boer attack at Bergendal in August 1900.

These were not the only Americans to fight for the Boers. Apart from those who had joined the Irish Brigade, there were others who simply joined their local commando. After Botha's Natal campaign, John Hassell, an American who had been fighting with the Vryheid commando, formed a small unit of American Scouts which was said by the Boers to be the strangest body of men in

31. Officers of the Irish Brigade outside Ladysmith. The senior officer, Colonel Blake, is wearing a white jacket.

the war. Howard Hilegas, a reporter for the *New York World*, wrote about a Pennsylvanian, John King, who was working on the mines when the war started. He and his best friend decided to fight in opposing armies. At the battle of Spionkop, King, the 'Boer', captured his 'British' friend and, after a brief conversation and a farewell grasp of the hand, shot him dead. Hilegas records that there were 300 Americans in the Boer army at various times. The one most valued by the Boers (apart from Colonel Blake) was Otto von Lossberg from Louisiana. He had received military training in Germany, where he was born, and commanded the guns under Piet de Wet at Sannah's Post, a crucial battle of the war.

The overseas members of the Irish Brigade entered the Transvaal through the port of Delagoa Bay in Portuguese territory. Although blockaded by the British navy, it was the only harbour open to the Boers. A British consul who reported on the movements of the Irish nationalists in Lourenço Marques later became an Irish nationalist martyr. His name was Roger Casement. At the time he was against the Boers because of their anti-black views, having already been campaigning against the exploitation of the blacks in the Congo.

At the beginning of the war foreigners were surprised to find the Boers so well prepared. But after Pretoria was captured the Boers went through a time of depression and disorganization which was so disheartening that many of the burghers went home, and the majority of the foreigners left the country. The Irish Brigade broke up in September 1900. MacBride went to Europe. However, there were a few who remained with the Boers, including Blake, who fought with the 'bitter-enders' until 1902.

In January 1900, however, a second Irish Brigade had been formed by an Australian, Arthur Lynch. Three quarters of its men were not Irish, and Davitt says that they included French, Germans, Dutch, Austrians, Greeks, Bulgarians, Italians and Americans. The reason they did not simply join Blake's force lies with Lynch himself. The Irish connection came from his father, who was from County Clare. After graduating from Melbourne University Lynch went to Europe to study. Later he worked as a journalist in London, where he became involved in Irish nationalist politics, trying unsuccessfully to get elected to the Westminster parliament as a candidate for Galway City. After moving back to Paris he was active among Irish expatriates. When the war started and anti-British feeling in France reached a peak, he was sent to the Transvaal as a correspondent of *Le Journal*. There he got the idea of starting a second Irish Brigade, perhaps as a stepping-stone to a political career. Richard Ruda, who wrote an authoritative account of the Transvaal Irish brigades, suggests that the decision lay 'more in the domain of Lynch's personal ambition and delusions of grandeur' than in a commitment to the Boer cause.[4]

32. Decorated butts of Boer rifles confiscated by the authorities in Dublin after the 1916 uprising.

Lynch's unit failed to take part in any major action before it broke up in July 1900. In recent years he has been called a Boer patriot, although in fact he did little for them. The idea really came about because of his treatment by the British for his nationalist activities after he left Africa. In June 1902 he was arrested while travelling through England. By then he had managed to get a seat in parliament, having won a by-election in November the previous year. He was convicted of high treason for his services to the Boers, and gained the distinction of being the last man to be sentenced by a British judge to be hanged, drawn and quartered. The sentence was later commuted to life imprisonment after President Roosevelt had intervened personally. Later he was released. He does not seem to have deserved all the fuss; his subsequent career was not distinguished. In the Irish National Library, amongst the papers of John Devoy, a leader of the Irish Republican Brotherhood or 'Fenians', is a written statement which purports to be about Lynch's activities in the war. Unfortunately it is not signed, but with it is a letter perhaps written by Higgins, one of the volunteers in MacBride's Brigade. It includes the following:

In the course of the second year of the Boer War I was detached, by order of the Transvaal Government, from MacBride's Irish Brigade, which was then taking part in the siege of Ladysmith and the fighting on the Tugela River, to investigate wholesale horse thefts and other looting then going on. The horses were stolen from the front and sent by train to Johannesburg or Pretoria, where they were sold by auction in the public market, and the Government bought them back for use in the field. There were also mules and wagons stolen. The money was sent to the horse thieves. The other loot was stored in a house in Johannesburg.

I traced the horse thefts to Lynch and I found rolls of silk, tweed, jewellery and other goods in Lynch's tent at Dundee. I met Lynch at the Glencoe railroad station, charged him with stealing horses and threatened to shoot him if I found him stealing any more. I made a full report of what I had found to the Boer Government.[5]

Lynch left the country soon afterwards.

HELP FROM THE EMPIRE

The Boer War was the first major campaign in which Britain received important military support from the colonies, particularly New Zealand, Canada and Australia. Help had been offered before war broke out, but had been refused. All three countries sent units as soon as the fighting started. The first Canadian contingent arrived in Cape Town at the end of November 1899 and was soon followed by a second. Nearly 3,000 volunteered, making up four contingents in all. The most useful were mounted infantry, such as the regiment which was raised by Lord Strathcona. They took part in a number of battles, but it was at Paardeberg, where they lost 118 men, that the Canadians distinguished themselves. A smaller contingent came from New Zealand during the first few weeks, trickling across in ten shiploads.

Australia sent two contingents, which, although short of experience, rapidly proved their worth. By the end there were more than 28,000 in South Africa. Soldiers from all three countries fought well in spite of their relative lack of experience. Australia was not yet federated and the provinces sent separate contingents. It was Australia which had taken the closest interest in the political situation before the war, partly because there were many Australians working on the Rand gold mines. There was even an Australian on the Uitlander Reform Committee in Johannesburg. A tradition had already been built up of sending Australian troops to fight with the imperial army. This had happened in the Maori War of 1867 and in the Sudan in 1885. As early as July 1899 Queensland offered a unit of mounted infantry to help in the Cape, and when war became inevitable, all the Australian governments passed resolutions to send volunteers. The decision was greeted with great enthusiasm and excited crowds saw the ships off.

Three months after the fighting began, the British suffered three serious defeats in one week. 'Black Week' had an immediate effect on the army. New volunteer regiments, such as London's City Imperial Yeomanry, sprang up overnight. Numerous unofficial organizations got in on the act. A committee of 'Influential and Patriotic Gentlemen' began competing with government agencies

to buy horses and equipment. The War Office set up a recruiting office in the Strand, and depots throughout the country were soon surrounded by long queues. War funds were started. Private companies of volunteers with names like The Duke of Cambridge's Own, Paget's Horse or Lovett's Scouts sprang up, supported by well-known personalities and sometimes even paid for by them. Other groups of volunteers had more humble origins. The historian Richard Cobb records that his father, Francis Hills Cobb, formed his own unit. At the outbreak of war he was working as a civil engineer in Peterborough and, after hearing a recruiting speech from Lord Roberts, volunteered with his clerks to form a company for the Royal Engineers. Some of the photographs he took during the guerilla war have been used in this book.

Another new phenomenon was the major help offered locally. In South Africa, English-speaking loyalists volunteered in large numbers. Police and Mounted Rifles from the Cape could have

33. Men of the first Canadian contingent leaving for South Africa.

34. Troops of the Australian contingent marching through Melbourne.

been used to block the first invasions, but were split up and posted for police duties with the first 5,000 volunteer reservists to be called up. Soon, however, the volunteer regiments' usefulness became accepted. The best, such as the Imperial Light Horse, did excellent work during the war. In the early days the Muslim and black communities offered help, but the British government and the Cape administration decided against using them for actual fighting. In December 1899, however, when things were really bad, about 6,000 blacks and coloureds were held in readiness in the Cape.

In the end the colonial regiments became an important and interesting feature of the war. Most were constituted as mounted infantry, a type of force which proved increasingly effective against the Boers as the war progressed. Originally conceived as purely colonial units, they were joined before long by Britons who came to Africa to fight. Many were officers from British regiments

which had not been ordered to Africa; by taking extended leave or resigning a commission they hoped to get fighting experience. The mixture of members of different social classes from Britain with colonials described by the officers in the new regiments as having been brought up free of caste and class was in every way beneficial. It resulted in an independence amongst irregulars which was shocking to officers of the regular army. At first most commissions in the new regiments were given to professional soldiers. But in the course of the war others went to men not from the usual officer class who, although without previous training, were found to have a talent for command. In the regular army these would have had little or no chance of promotion.

The pity is that this practice was not immediately adopted by regular regiments. The irregular units had been specifically created for service against the Boers, and when the war ended they were disbanded in Africa or incorporated into the South African army after Union. Their effect on the upper levels of the British army was delayed until the Second World War, when some officers with experience in them achieved high command. Although Boer tactics had been adopted at regimental level throughout the British army,

35. Men of the 53rd Company of Imperial Yeomanry. Colonial and even Imperial troops came to look more like Boers as the war went on. This was particularly irritating to the Boers, who complained that they could be shot if found in British uniforms.

during the First World War senior staff officers like French and Haig still held to the nineteenth-century principle of complete separation between officers and men. It is also significant that the idea of war by attrition was very foreign to Boer and colonial alike. It is tempting to speculate that if the war in Europe had been delayed ten years, millions of British corpses might not now lie in French earth.

By the end of the Boer War more than eighty irregular units had been created. The best known and perhaps the most effective was Rimington's Scouts, known as 'Tigers' because of the band of wild-cat fur they wore round their hats. Most were colonials who knew the country well and could speak Dutch and some African languages. They fought in almost every campaign, at first usually as scouts attached to regular regiments, but later as a unit. Their commanding officer, Major Michael Frederick Rimington,

36. Colonel Rimington and his 'Tigers'.

was a remarkable man. Tall and distinguished with turned-up moustaches, he was said to have been knocked about so much by hunting and polo accidents that he had a lopsided look and leaned slightly to one side as he walked. He was the first officer to use mounted infantry like a Boer commando. His activities as a guide formed the basis of the ideas subsequently elaborated by Baden-Powell after the war, and he was certainly much more successful at this type of warfare than 'B-P'. The attitude of the regular army to these irregulars was a problem. They were often blamed for the early Boer ambushes, and talk about spies and traitors amongst Rimington's men was reported from the ranks. The regulars were not nearly as suspicious of the Empire troops from Canada, New Zealand and Australia.

The Australians were particularly hated by the Boers, who could not understand why a nation which possessed a pioneer spirit and a dislike of foreign authority very similar to their own could support British imperialism. These attitudes certainly existed among Australian troops and did not endear them to British officers. Much has been written about Breaker Morant and other Australian officers who were sentenced to death for shooting prisoners. His story is not typical in any way – for one thing he was not an Australian. However, some Australians did get into trouble with the authorities. In May 1901 a recently arrived contingent of Victorians on their way to the front by train

made very free comments on the appearance of a staff-officer who happened to be standing on the platform. Hearing their remarks, he ordered them back into their trucks, whereupon they flatly refused to go. In the end they obeyed the order of their own major. When asked by him why they had behaved in so unsoldierlike a manner, they answered that the staff-officer had 'no right to give them commands'. 'We are Australians,' they said, 'not Tommies, and have our own officers.'[6]

Worse was to follow. The following month, while operating under Beatson's column, the same troops were attacked at night by Commandant Muller, a highly experienced veteran. Within minutes twenty were dead and forty wounded. The remainder surrendered and were stripped of uniforms and weapons, and a large convoy of rifles and ammunition, including pom-pom shells, was captured. Beatson learned of the attack from a few who escaped and immediately set out to help. He arrived at dawn and was incensed to hear that they had been attacked while eating round campfires and that the barest minimum of sentries had been posted: 'We were telling yarns and talking of things in general when suddenly, without warning, a most terrific fire was opened upon us.' Beatson was partly to blame for what happened. Mustering the men, who had not recovered completely from their ordeal, he hurled abuse at them, calling them 'a lot of wasters and white-livered curs', adding that all Australians were alike. When

37. Baden-Powell was called 'bathing towel' by his men.

38 (*left*). Newly arrived British officers. In the middle is Lieutenant Speyer whose diary of his experiences as ADC to Kitchener's brother Frank is now in the Royal Army Museum with albums of his photographs.

39 (*above*). British officers in the field. Uniforms became more and more eccentric as the war progressed.

he noticed that an officer was taking notes he is reported to have said, 'You can add "dogs" too.' The ringleaders of the mutiny which followed were arrested, court-martialled and sentenced to death. An outcry ensued and Kitchener commuted their sentences to three years' imprisonment. They were subsequently pardoned after representations from Australia to the British government.

The Boer War has been called a gentlemen's war. If there is any truth in this idea, it is because both armies respected each other. There were remarkably few of the atrocities we have come to expect in the latter half of the twentieth century. Both sides learned a great deal from the war, the British army being particularly affected by its experience. Even the old guard respected the Boers. With characteristic insight Haig, then a cavalry officer, called these hard-bitten veterans 'the sportsmen of the veld'. His personal servant, Sergeant T. Secrett, records him as saying: 'When this wretched business ends I only hope I have the opportunity to join them in a shooting expedition, or play polo with some of their brilliant riders.'[7]

3.   THE INJURED

In the Boer War both sides went to great trouble to look after their wounded, but the combatants also benefited from the fact that rifles were not then designed to inflict massive damage. The effect of a bullet passing through human tissue depends not only on its velocity but also on whether it tumbles or wobbles in flight. Today anti-personnel weapons are designed to cause maximum injury. Bullets can be made to pitch and yaw so violently that even non-explosive types will cause flesh to disintegrate when penetrated. By contrast, the high-velocity rifles in use at the turn of the century were intended to kill cleanly. They were finely machined, hurling bullets in such a straight trajectory that wounds were often very localized. The typical bullet wound of the Boer War looked like a small bruise with a central entry hole, whereas the corresponding weapon of today can cause the loss of half a victim's chest. The German Mauser rifle in particular produced remarkably clean wounds, its hard-cased bullets often passing straight through the body. They could, however, be made more dangerous. British troops reported that 'dum-dum' and even explosive bullets were used by the Boers. Dum-dums were either made of soft lead which spread out on impact, or were fashioned on the battlefield by cutting through the hard outer-case of a standard bullet. Both sides used them, but it was not common practice.

During the early weeks of the war the Boers were accused of using poisoned bullets which were said to cause particularly nasty infected wounds. From time to time the story still appears in modern books. In the museum of the Dorset Regiment one of the old cabinets contains a clip of five Boer Mauser bullets, labelled as 'poisoned'. Unfortunately the clip has been polished so often that analysis of any chemical on the surface is unlikely to be productive. It seems likely that the story began when captured Boer bullets were found to be coated with green fat, used to lubricate the chamber and barrel of the rifle.

Wounds were often described as being painless at first. Men who had been shot commonly reported that it felt like being pushed, or tapped with a hammer. Lynch, who wrote some of the best accounts of the fighting in his *Impressions of a War Correspondent*, makes the following observations:

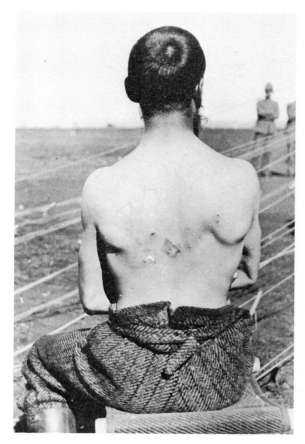 

40. Front and back view of a soldier soon after receiving a Mauser bullet-wound through the chest.

Death from a Mauser bullet is less painful than the drawing of a tooth. Such at least appears to be the case, speaking generally from apparent evidence, without having the opportunity of collecting the opinions of those who have actually died. In books we have read of shrieks of expiring agony; but ask those who have been on many battle-fields, and they will not tell you they have heard them. As a rule a sudden exclamation 'I'm hit!', 'My God!', 'Damn it'. They look as if staggering from the blow of a fist rather than from a tiny pencil of lead – then sudden paleness, perhaps a grasping of the hands occasionally as if to hold on to something, when the bottom seems to be falling out of all things stable, but generally no signs of ought else than the dulling of death – dulling to sleep – a drunken death that it often seems – very commonplace as a rule.[8]

There were, of course, many who suffered terribly, especially when it was impossible to get them out of the firing zone, although both sides behaved very well to the wounded. This was the experience of a British sergeant at the Siege of Ladysmith:

As the morning came, firing was very heavy and two Boers were shooting over the very rock behind which I lay ... As the sun rose, the heat became intense and my wound gave me anxiety and pain and I could not stop the bleeding. I took the puttee off my right leg and tied it tightly above the left knee and tried to stop the dripping but without avail as I was in such a cramped position. However, I found that the blood on the ground had congealed with the intense heat. As a last resource, on seeing this, I undid my puttee and boot and put my foot in the sun and to my great relief my ankle became one clot of blood – the bleeding had ceased.

By this time the heat was intense and my thirst more so; in fact, it became so bad that I had to place my finger on my tongue to hold it down to get my breath. Before this I had appealed to the two Boers who were firing over my head to give a drink of water. At last, one of them who had a short beard handed me his water bottle – which was a British one – what relief I got from that drink! To my intense sorrow ... on handing back the bottle and while he was putting the strap round his neck, my unknown benefactor was shot through the face and disappeared from my sight with the blood gushing from his mouth.[9]

Medical attention was prompt and efficient. The Royal Army Medical Corps had been formed as a result of a public outcry against the terrible suffering of the troops in the Crimea. A comprehensive system of treatment was introduced, and the Boer War really tested its worth. The pay of medical corps soldiers was increased and their training improved; they were given equal rank and status with those in fighting units. Training of medical officers also improved as the influence of the new Army Medical School spread through the service.

Surgery had made dramatic progress during the last half of the nineteenth century and the RAMC took full advantage of this, so that by 1899 army surgery was based on the most modern concepts of the time. Lister's 'antisepsis', with carbolic solutions which killed germs, had gradually been replaced by aseptic surgery, in which sterilized equipment is used and great care taken to avoid the introduction of germs. General anaesthesia was standard for all operations. At the beginning of the Boer War the Professor of Military Surgery at the Army Medical School was Surgeon-General Stevenson. It was a measure of the war's importance that he joined Lord Roberts's army as Principal Medical Officer.

The RAMC was well established by 1899. Thus most doctors who served in South Africa were professional soldiers, but the army also recruited a number of civilian specialist surgeons. At least seven such consultants were appointed, including such famous British surgeons as Sir William MacCormac, Watson Cheyne, William Stokes (who died in South Africa), Kendal Franks and G.L. Cheatle, as well as Sir Thomas Fitzgerald from Australia. Dr Washbourne of the Imperial Yeomanry Hospital was appointed as a consultant physician. The most famous surgeon who went to South Africa was Sir Frederick Treves, who has recently come once again to public attention as the benefactor of the poor deformed 'Elephant Man', for whom he arranged shelter in the London Hospital where he worked. Treves was an excellent surgeon, and also a writer of some distinction. He worked in a Field Hospital during Buller's exploits in Natal and later published a moving account of his experiences, *The Tale of a Field Hospital*, partly based on articles written at the time for the *British Medical Journal*. Most of the London consultants spent only a few months in Africa: it was difficult for a well-known surgeon to leave Harley Street for longer than that without losing his practice. They were, however, well paid. L.S. Amery states in the authoritative *Times History of the War in South Africa* that in 1900 the army was paying consultant surgeons £5,000 a year.[10]

The surgeon who made the biggest name for himself in the war was George Henry Makins of St Thomas's Hospital. In 1901 he published a textbook of military surgery which is now a classic. It includes an exhaustive survey of the injuries caused by small-calibre bullets and gives authoritative figures for casualty rates and mortality. For example, the casualty rate amongst the 15,000 troops who took part in the relief of Kimberley was just over 12 per cent, while mortality amongst the wounded was only 2 per cent. This compared very favourably with the situation in previous British campaigns, but the figures conceal the high casualty rate of officers. Later in the war most surgery was carried out by regular army surgeons, whose results were just as good by all accounts.

Of the 22,000 soldiers treated for injuries during the war, most survived if they had been taken to a first-aid post without delay, for surgical teams were never overwhelmed with casualties. This contrasts strongly with the plight of the 54,800 injured at Gettysburg in the American Civil War, some of whom are said to have starved on the battlefield because there were not enough stretcher-bearers. Reflecting the contemporary view that a European war was unlikely in the near future, RAMC plans were geared to moving casualties vast distances from outposts of the Empire which were in a constant state of unrest. As early as 1883 arrangements existed for the removal of the wounded from a battle zone, their surgical care and their eventual evacuation to England.

The disposal of casualties was to be accomplished in stages. Battalion doctors were stationed on the battlefield. Wounded men who could be moved were to be taken to a dressing station by one of the two bearer companies attached to each division. From there they would go to one of four nearby mobile field ambulances where more complex operations could be carried out. Patients would then be transferred to one of the eight stationary divisional hospitals set up at twenty-mile intervals along the line of communication. When an injured man was well enough he would move to a base hospital. If his injury prevented him returning to his unit, he would be shipped to Portsmouth or to a military hospital in England before being sent back to his unit or discharged. During the Boer War 22,000 troops were treated for battle wounds or accidental injuries. The Medical Department of the army mobilized 151 staff and regimental units for the African campaign. There were twenty-eight field ambulances, five stationary hospitals and sixteen general hospitals. A number of voluntary organizations also set up medical units such as hospitals, hospital ships (like the one in which Churchill's mother visited the Cape), field ambulances and first-aid posts.

In addition to the bearer companies attached to field units, there were more than a thousand Indians, mostly from Natal, who had organized themselves as non-combatants to carry men off the battlefield. Mahatma Ghandi, then practising as a lawyer in Dur-

41. Indian stretcher-bearers from Natal.

42. Bringing the wounded down from Spionkop hill the morning after the battle.

ban, volunteered for this work – motivated, as he explains in his autobiography, by loyalty as a British citizen – and was present at the battles of Colenso and Spionkop. His unit was trained by an English doctor named Booth. A second unit was set up by Johannesburg and Cape Town Jews, and helped both the Boer and the British armies at a number of engagements.

In the first battles, stretcher-bearers would walk into the firing zone as soon as a man had been wounded and carry him straight off the field. It was even quite common for soldiers taking part in the battle to carry off the injured. This practice ceased when it was realized that the Boers continued firing at anything that moved. Thereafter it became more of an ordeal to be wounded, especially if the fighting went on until sundown. It was almost impossible to find casualties in the dark.

In the dry African veld, wounds given rapid treatment healed quickly without infection. The widespread use of field dressings (carried by every soldier and to be applied as soon as possible after injury) also helped. These had been introduced by the Prussians in 1884, and consisted of a sterile gauze pad stitched to a bandage and covered with waterproofing, later removed to allow the wound to dry. Each pack contained two dressings and a number of safety pins. Later in the war men were often injured far from medical attention, and it might be days before they could see a doctor. Infection then became much more of a hazard. On 29 April 1901 Frederick Porter, a regular medical officer who kept one of the best diaries of the war, wrote:

> Poor Stanley arrived about 7 p.m. He was very excited and a bit delirious. We looked at the limb and found that the same sort of gangrene which had affected the hip [case] had attacked this, and spread right up the leg and to the abdomen. There was no use in dressing it. I asked him if he would like to know the truth about the matter, and he said he would. I then told him that he would die in a few hours and that nothing could save him. He took it like a man and told Brooke, his brother officer, some messages to give to his mother and people. Up to this time he felt he was going to get well, so that it must have come as a great blow to him.[11]

Primary surgical care was undertaken in the field ambulances. Conditions were nearly always difficult in the bell-tent operating theatres because of heat, dust, wind and flies. Although their equipment was limited, surgeons often carried out major operations. The main difference between civilian and battle surgery is that military surgeons can be faced with more patients than they can deal with. This is still true today, and was certainly a feature of many nineteenth-century wars, in which most armies had only a handful of doctors attached to fighting units. However, in the Boer War, although at times the medical service was hard-pressed, the number of injured men was never overwhelming. The first principle of surgical treatment in battle is to sort the wounded into three categories: those who are lightly wounded and need no immediate attention other than pain relief; those whose wounds are so severe that survival is impossible or unlikely, who are simply given morphia; and finally the group on whom most effort will be concentrated – those with injuries which, although life-threatening, are curable. Lives are saved by making sure that patients with head and neck injuries can breathe, by stopping haemorrhage caused by damage to large arteries, and by closing open chest wounds. In spite of all the modern advances in surgery, this system of sorting and first aid for casualties – known as 'triage' – is still in use. More complicated or expert surgery is left to better equipped hospitals down the line, though it is agonizing when a surgeon must decide against treating a patient, and many have been haunted by such memories for years afterwards.

Operations on flesh wounds worked on the time-honoured principle of 'debridement', which consists of removing all dead tissue that looks as if it might have been damaged. The wound is then left open and dressed. When one first sees a surgeon with war experience cutting away large chunks of skin and muscle round a wound, it seems a crude and unnecessarily damaging procedure. But if the injured tissues are not removed, or swollen flesh is sewn

43. Field ambulance at the Battle of Belmont (1899): wounded waiting for treatment.

44. Field ambulance at the Battle of Belmont: surgeons dressing wounds.

together, infection is common. Worse, gas gangrene may infect the dead muscle. Surgeons without experience of war find all this hard to believe, and it is said to be a lesson which has to be learned again and again in each war.

General anaesthesia was surprisingly good, and by the time of the Boer War was being used for all operations. The report of the 6th General Hospital states:

Chloroform has proved itself to be the only practical form of anaesthetic in this dry climate. Ether was used on many occasions and proved unsatisfactory owing to rapid evaporation. A supply of nitrous oxide gas to a general hospital would have proved to be of inestimable value in minor surgical operations of which there were a large number, and would have

45. Minor casualties after the Battle of Belmont.

46. Surgeon in a tent operating on a patient's neck. Rubber gloves were not used until 1904. The anaesthetic was usually chloroform dripped on to a mask over the patient's face.

avoided the inevitable risks attached to chloroform anaesthesia. For ten months anaesthesia had been freely administered daily without any untoward effects, but in one week in November 1900 two deaths occurred during chloroform administration.[12]

One important difference between surgical practice in the Boer War and in subsequent wars lay in the treatment of shock due to blood loss. Lancing only discovered the main blood groups in 1902; without this knowledge blood transfusion was highly dangerous. In fact there was no military blood transfusion service until the 1914–18 War. The treatment of shock was primitive:

I wanted to pump in strychnine as before, but Cheyne was playing about with 3 or 4 drop doses. The man was very bad and looked like dying so I got 10 drops and gave it. He was astonished and said that it was a very big dose, but I said that he wanted it. Then he thought that he would try transfusion, and put one and a half pints of salt water into a vein.[13]

The intravenous infusion of saline, even in large amounts, will not save the life of a patient who has lost a great deal of blood. Many

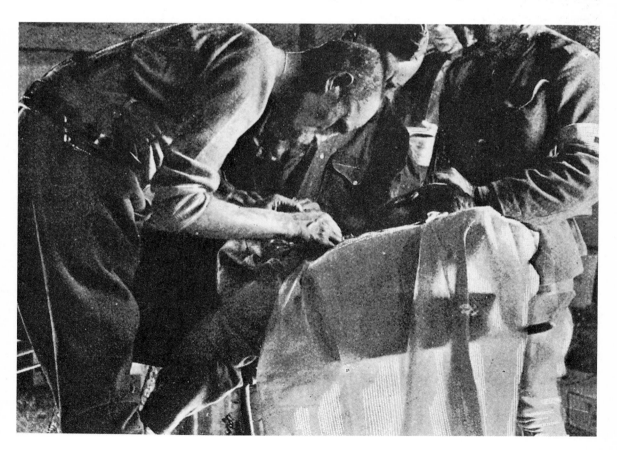

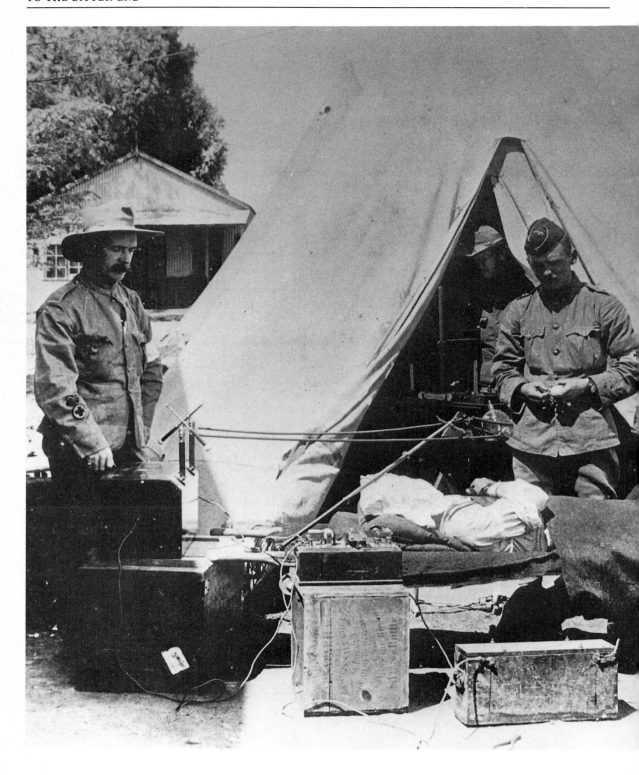

47 (*left*). Early portable X-ray machine used at Ladysmith.

48 (*above*). X-ray showing retained Mauser bullet behind hip-joint. The bone is not fractured.

died from haemorrhage. Here, however, is a description of what could be achieved by a brave surgeon:

They had a case who had been put on [the hospital train] yesterday and he had been bleeding badly. They put him under chloroform and plugged the wound in the thigh, but the oozing went on. The man in charge didn't like to take him on as he thought he might die, so we had to take him off. We brought him to camp and put him on the operating table, which we had to rig up in a bell-tent. Half the wall had to be turned back so as to give us room to work, so it was practically in the open air. Under chloroform (given by the Life Guards doctor) we found that the thigh was smashed up near the head, so there was no alternative but amputation through the hip joint. It was a desperate remedy, but there was nothing else. I started (it was the first time I had ever done it) and got the anterior flap by transfixing. I couldn't get the head of the bone out, for there was only a small bit of the shaft left, and Tate couldn't control the bleeding from the forward artery owing to its being so muscular. I therefore plugged the posterior part of the wound with swabs that I had made at Maitland Camp, and tied all the vessels in the anterior flap with strong silk that I had brought with me. It was lucky that I had it, for there was not a bit of silk fit for use in the equipment and I don't known what I should have done otherwise. Just as I had cut the posterior flap his heart began to fail, so I injected strychnine in large doses. I had to finish the operation in a hurry, but it was a good success as far as the shape and size of the flap go. In about an hour I had given him 13 drops of solution of strychnine, which would have poisoned an ordinary man, and he rallied in great style. I got a quart of champagne from the Colonel of the Inskillings for him but he wouldn't drink it.[14]

Wounds of the soft tissues of the body were well treated, but more complicated injuries could be a problem. However, in some specialized areas of surgery, great advances had taken place by 1900. Many injuries involved damage to bone, such as a compound or open fracture, and these cases were also treated by debridement, after which the wound was packed. The limb was then immobilized in some sort of splint, in much the same way as was done in the First and Second World Wars. In this campaign special splints were supplied, which were made of canvas with strips of bamboo sewn on to keep them rigid. Plaster of Paris was also available and was often used after the bone had been set. It had been introduced by the French in 1851, and by the end of the century the standard way to immobilize a fracture was for the surgeon himself to impregnate bandages with it and apply them over cotton-wool after dipping them in water. Traction was also used, particularly in the fixed hospitals. The treatment of fractures had been vastly improved by the introduction of X-rays. Although it was only in 1895 that Roentgen discovered X-rays, they were already in use by British army doctors in the Egyptian campaign of 1898. At least nine X-ray machines were taken to South Africa for the war. The images produced by even the most primitive

49. Soldiers who had survived surgical treatment of head wounds.

apparatus were very helpful in finding bullets which had remained inside the body.

Head injuries were quite often treated in this war, even if the brain had been damaged. Charles Veal, whose diary is now in the National Army Museum in London, received such a wound at the Battle of Paardeberg:

I was in the third line under Major Ball, who presently came along to me. We lay down for a little in a shallow dip in the ground and discussed the situation until we came to the conclusion that our particular Boer was making remarkably good but unpleasant shooting at us. We hunted for him in the bushes through our glasses and at last I saw a suspicious object up a tree. As the officers were only armed with a carbine, I luckily turned to borrow a rifle from Sergeant Phelps or some other man near, when I received my quietus in the shape of a bullet through the head. Major Ball came to the rescue at once and was extremely good and by his smartness I believe I was saved from bleeding to death. Westmacott [?], who was further along the line, sent his stretcher and bearers over and they quickly and pluckily stood there whilst I was hustled onto the stretcher and carried out of immediate danger. I was nearly suffocated with blood when I lay down and the sun (and I must confess – fright) did not at all improve matters . . .

After much halting and deliberation we struck a doctor who was very kind and advised me to push on to the main hospital . . .

50. Volunteer nurses in Lichtenberg (1901): Sister Faith (standing), Sister Gertie (sitting).

A short time afterwards we reached the hospital which consisted of an operating marquee and a few wagons and bell-tents. A Wesleyan parson took me off the horse and produced some brandy and beef tea which I gulped down with the greatest relief. Shortly afterwards I was taken into the operating tent and put on the table. Two doctors there shook their heads and thought my case was too bad to trouble about with all the cases still waiting. But a remark, unfit for publication, from me changed their minds, and in a few minutes I was all patched up and had great notches cut out of my beautiful scarlet head.[15]

On the other hand, the treatment of chest injuries, a common cause of death in battle, was quite inadequate. The management of abdominal wounds also proved a great disappointment. By the time the war began abdominal operations were frequently carried out in civilian practice, and most of the young surgeons hoped to use their experience in war conditions. The British Surgeon-General, W.F. Stevenson, originally tried to encourage military surgeons to undertake exploratory operations for wounds in this area. However, the difficulty of carrying out abdominal surgery on the battlefield and the bad results which followed made him change his mind, and an order was issued forbidding emergency operations on abdominal wounds. Lord Roberts's son, Fred, was wounded in the abdomen at the Battle of Colenso, having volunteered to rescue some cannon from within the Boer fire-zone. Bearers managed to get him to a field ambulance, but he died five days later. It was not until the First World War that abdominal operations on war casualties were undertaken routinely.

During Roberts's advance in 1900, newspapers in England published accounts of the army medical services in South Africa which were highly critical of the way the wounded were kept waiting for treatment. Roberts took the reports seriously and telegraphed the War Office to point out the difficulty he had in keeping open the railway line to Cape Town, along which the injured had to be moved. The line was nearly 900 miles long, and every bridge of the last 128 miles had been destroyed. In fact, the criticism was unfair. The standard of treatment was high, and the hospitals well run. Nurses who went to Africa were well trained in Florence Nightingale's methods. Some of the girls who volunteered came from the best families in England. Many had been recruited by voluntary organizations at the beginning of the war. A flood of young unattached men and women rushed out to Cape Town, eager to help in any way they could. From some accounts, however, the main attraction of South Africa was the social life in Cape Town. Far from parental eyes, the young people lived and played in a style more like the 1980s than the 1890s.

The medical attention received by injured Boers was of the same high standard. At the outbreak of war, medical equipment, doctors and nurses poured in from France, Holland, Germany and

51. Boer 'hospital'.

52. Boer field ambulance.

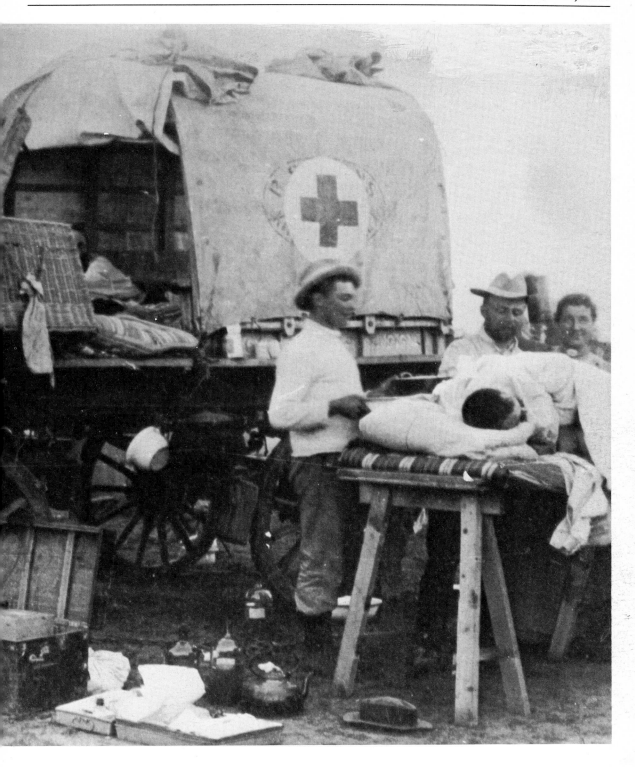

Russia. A Russian nursing sister, Sophia Izedinova, wrote a book about her experience with the Boers which has recently been translated and published in South Africa. A public fund had been set up in Russia in 1899. It collected a considerable amount of money and fitted out a hospital and an ambulance train with the help of the Dutch. The Russian Red Cross also offered ambulances to the British, but the offer was turned down. Many British soldiers were treated by Boer surgeons. When Lord Methuen was wounded and captured in the last weeks of the war, he was treated by Dr von Rennenkampf of De la Rey's staff. Lord Methuen's wound was a compound or open fracture of the thigh. He was treated with kindness by De la Rey, who sent him back to the British lines.

In one way the Boers had a much easier time than the British in arranging for the care of the injured: they were fighting in their own country. Considerable help was always available in the vicinity of a battle and any available building could be used as a hospital. Ambulances were attached to each commando. Porter visited one of them in March 1900:

> I went down in the afternoon and saw the Boer ambulance which was there. They had a house and several marquees which were in charge of two officers of the Dutch East Indian Army. There are several women nurses there, and 8 wounded ... What impressed me most was the Acetylene plant and lamps all over the house and marquees. Most of the appliances were from the French Red Cross.[16]

The types of wound the Boers received were similar to those suffered by British soldiers, with one exception. In a number of battles the British used lancers to chase the retreating enemy, for whom the consequences could be grave, as Porter reports:

> One Boer was struck by a lance. It is the only case I have ever seen, it went right through him and out at his chest and when pulled back it drew out a large piece of omentum from the abdomen. This I had to remove and I am rather curious to see how he got on.[17]

Later in the war conditions worsened for Boer casualties. Most units were able to maintain an ambulance service, but the majority of Boers wounded during the guerilla war were brought into the British lines for treatment.

The surgical facilities provided by the British army for the treatment of the wounded during the Boer War were vastly better than those available in previous campaigns. Unfortunately, similar advances had not been made in the prevention and treatment of war's attendant diseases. This was the last war in which more succumbed to disease than were killed in battle. But mortality among combatants was only a part of the overall toll. It was disease among Boer women and children in the concentration camps (dealt with in detail in Chapter 8) which became the main tragedy of the war.

4. NINETEENTH-CENTURY WAR

The war began with the Boers invading British territory at four points: into Natal in the east, towards Mafeking in the north-west of the Transvaal, in the direction of Kimberley in the south-west, and across the Orange river into the eastern Cape. A glance at the map reveals their strategy. All four invasion routes were directed at railway lines. Kimberley and Mafeking lay on the line which ran along the Transvaal's western border and connected Cape Town with Rhodesia. It was the best route to bring troops up through British territory to a spot from which Pretoria could easily be reached without having to cross major geographical boundaries. There were not enough troops in the Cape for an invasion to be expected imminently from that quarter, but reinforcements were on the way. The same applied to the railway line which ran between De Aar in the eastern Cape and Bloemfontein, and it also received branches from other ports where troops could be landed. In addition, both Kimberley and Mafeking were interesting to the Boers for reasons other than their strategic importance. Mafeking had been the starting place for Jameson's ill-fated raid. Kimberley not only contained the diamond fields but was the headquarters of Jameson's boss, Rhodes. What is more, Rhodes had not run away and still sat in the town, as tempting as a toy in a shop window.

However, it was not the Cape which was the centre of the Boer thrust. The main bulk of commandos from the Transvaal and the Free State invaded Natal, whose capture was the linchpin of their strategy. Ladysmith, the main town on the railway line to Durban, was the headquarters of the largest British force in South Africa. The movement of Sir George White's force from India to reinforce this garrison had precipitated the Boer ultimatum. White's troops arrived only just in time to prevent the Boers pushing straight on to Durban. He managed to hold their advance by throwing in all available men, including marines from Durban, their white tropical uniforms dyed with coffee. Guns were even taken off the battleships in Durban harbour. Sailors from HMS *Powerful* arrived with four 12-pounder cannons and two 94-pounder guns, just in time to take part in the Battle of Ladysmith. Their efficiency and

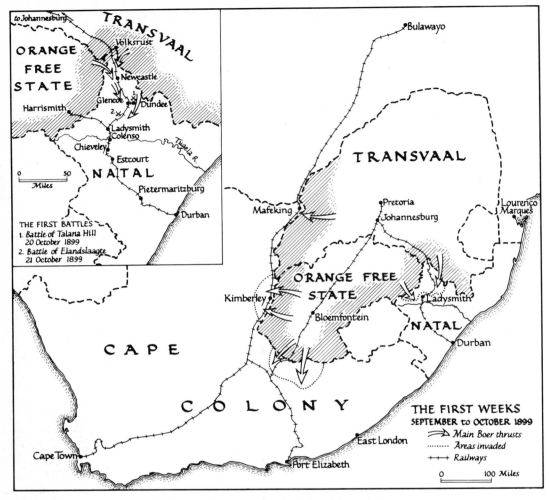

THE FIRST BATTLES
1. Battle of Talana Hill 20 October 1899
2. Battle of Elandslaagte 21 October 1899

THE FIRST WEEKS
SEPTEMBER to OCTOBER 1899
→ Main Boer thrusts
...... Areas invaded
+++++ Railways
0   100 Miles

speed is commemorated in the naval gun race which is still one of the main events of the Royal Tournament. Although White held the advance, the Boers soon surrounded Ladysmith, with its garrison of 12,000 troops.

In these first weeks battles were fought at Talana Hill on 20 October, at Elandslaagte the following day, and at Dundee on 23 October. Elandslaagte is the one best remembered in South Africa. When the Transvaalers retreated, General French (who was to be British commander in 1914) sent in his lancers. To the Boers, fighting with 'spears' was barbarous. Another feature of the battle was the high casualty rate on the Boer side, particularly in the foreign contingents. But the battles could not be called British victories; they too lost a considerable number of men, including the first field commander, Major-General Sir Penn Symons, who was shot at Dundee when he entered the zone of fire. Even when battles were apparently won and the Boers had retreated, they could be seen regrouping nearby. White ordered General Yule, who had replaced Symons, to fall back to Ladysmith when he learned that the Free Staters were advancing on the town. It was a bad move. Yule's column only managed to get to safety after a four days' difficult march in atrocious weather. On the 26th the Transvaal and Free State commandos joined hands. By the 30th the main British force in South Africa had been trapped in Ladysmith after a disastrous battle at Lombard's Kop near the town.

The Boers' marksmanship was an unwelcome surprise. Their ability to pick off British officers led to a general order that these should dress as private soldiers. But the disproportionate loss of officers continued. Imagine the excitment in Bloemfontein and Pretoria at the news that the 'Khakis' were retreating towards the sea, leaving nearly 700 dead and thousands of prisoners. Photographs of columns of captured soldiers flashed around the world. Their publication caused an outcry in Britain, where the public was not used to the idea of British troops surrendering. This had

53. Cecil Rhodes (in white trousers behind horse) in Kimberley during the siege.

not been a feature of nineteenth-century African and Indian campaigns, in which capture had often meant immediate execution.

The Boers were jubilant. They had retreated at Talana and Elandslaagte, but this was their usual tactic, and they had advanced again when the British moved back. In the Republics it was a moment of exhilaration. It seemed likely that with a little more effort the whole British army could be defeated before reinforcements arrived. But the Boers had already thrown away their advantage. Their original plan was to concentrate on a rapid strike to Durban, which would seal off the deep-water harbour there and prevent the British landing supplies and reinforcements within reach of the Transvaal. The other prong of their attack was aimed at capturing the pass through the Hex River mountains near Cape Town. For the British to regain this would involve a direct frontal attack, which, if it proved possible at all, would be costly and dangerous. But, instead of following this plan, old Commandant-General Joubert frittered away the chance of victory by concentrating on the besieged towns, which he should have left to be dealt with after the main objectives had been achieved.

54. Officer (right) wearing ranker's uniform in accordance with a general order aimed at reducing officers' high casualty rate. Porter (see n. 11) wrote on 21 November 1899: 'They are trying to render the officer less distinctive; all medal ribbons to be taken off, Sam Brown belts under the jacket, buttons dulled, also scabbards. Infantry officers' swords are to be taken away and they are to carry carbines . . . All the pipeclay has been taken off the men's belts and haversacks are being stained with Condy's fluid.'

55. Churchill in captivity (Pretoria, 1899).

Deneys Reitz, who wrote the best Boer diary of the war, records a moment at the battle for Ladysmith when White's whole column, sent out to push back the Boers, was suddenly seen to be retreating back into the town across an empty plain. De Wet, one of the new commandants, who had played a crucial role in capturing a British column that morning, was heard to mutter angrily, 'Los jou ruiters; los jou ruiters' ('Send in your riders'). Joubert refused, quoting a Dutch proverb, 'When God holds out a finger, do not take the whole hand.'

A news story which made headlines during the first weeks was the capture of a young officer, Winston Churchill, who had taken leave from his regiment to report for the *Morning Post*. On 15 November he went on an armoured train sent out to reconnoitre the line north of Estcourt, where Boer patrols had been reported. These were sighted near Chieveley and the train was ordered back, but before it could get away the Boers began firing. The train increased speed, turned a corner and smashed into a rock which had been placed on the tracks. The first truck was flung into the air, spilling troops in all directions; the second, an armoured

56. Churchill free: on board a ship
going back to Durban after escaping.

57. Churchill the politician; making
an impromptu speech in Durban after
his escape.

wagon, was thrown on its side; the third became wedged half off
the tracks. Young Churchill wrote, 'We were not long left in the
comparative peace and safety of a railway accident.'[18]

In the brisk action which followed, Churchill played a heroic
and widely reported role in freeing the trapped rear of the train
so that it managed to get away. As the train started moving,
however, he jumped off and was captured. The Boers, gloating at
having caught the son of a famous British politician, were soon
dismayed when he escaped from the State Model School in Pretoria, which was being used as a prison, and a reward was offered
for his capture. After hiding in a coalmine he reached Portuguese
territory and caught a ship from Lourenço Marques back to Durban. He arrived on 23 December to a hero's welcome. This ad-
venture, which became front-page news all over the world,
launched his public career, and was a great help in his subsequent
election success.

The more one reads the descriptions of the event, the more likely it seems that Churchill allowed himself to be captured. Why not? It was the action of a master journalist. In later years he told Botha that he recognized him as the 'bearded Boer' who made the capture. Botha smiled politely. It made an excellent story and cemented their friendship, but it is very unlikely to be true. Over the years many Boers claimed the distinction, but it probably belonged to a burgher from the Krugersdorp commando named Chris van Veijeren. Until his death in 1966 Veijeren continued to insist, in letters to newspapers and in sworn documents, that he was the 'bearded Boer' who had captured Churchill.[19]

The first weeks were a shock in Britain, but the Tory government did not panic. There had been many a campaign in which Britain had been caught unprepared, only to recover as soon as the army was allowed to send a force adequate to the situation. That force was already on its way.

BULLER'S CAMPAIGN

British territory in South Africa had been invaded because the local garrison had not been adequately reinforced, and the initial fighting had gone against the British army; now a task force of ships containing a full army corps was dispatched to deal with the threat. There was no regular army available and a large number of reservists had to be called up.

It was on the day White landed in Durban that the newly formed Committee of National Defence issued orders for this mobilization. The corps consisted of one cavalry and three infantry divisions, and more than 100 guns. The force contained volunteers from Canada, the Australian states and New Zealand. Meanwhile nearly 5,000 volunteers in Natal were formed into mounted regiments. On 20 October, after a few weeks of organizational difficulties, the first troops embarked at Southampton. They travelled in a vast convoy of merchant ships under the watchful eye of the Royal Navy's Channel Squadron. When the convoy reached Gibraltar, eight battleships took over the patrol for the journey to the Canaries. The Naval Command received a report that a foreign cruiser had been sighted and took the threat seriously. A strict black-out was maintained and the convoy altered course and sailed well west of the usual trade route. There was a lot to protect. Nearly 60,000 tons of merchant ships had been recruited as transport. The British Empire was very wealthy in those days, and the press in England reported with some pride that the diversion of these ships from civilian trade had hardly affected the cost of freight.

Sir Redvers Buller, who had been in charge of the Aldershot

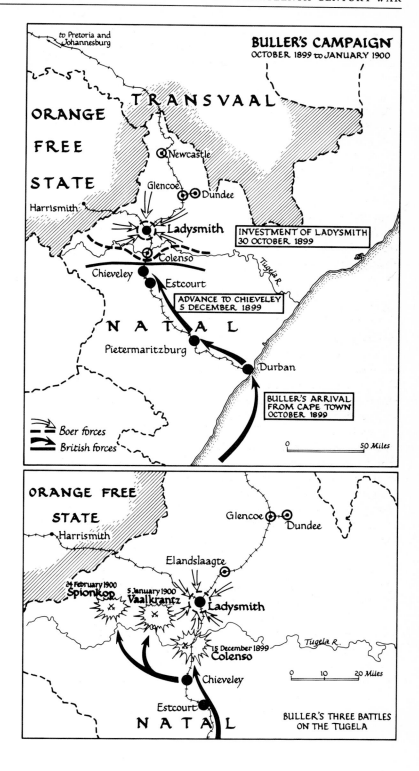

BULLER'S CAMPAIGN
OCTOBER 1899 to JANUARY 1900

to Pretoria and Johannesburg

ORANGE

FREE

STATE

TRANSVAAL

Newcastle

Glencoe
Dundee

Harrismith

Ladysmith

INVESTMENT OF LADYSMITH
30 OCTOBER 1899

Colenso

Chieveley

Estcourt

ADVANCE TO CHIEVELEY
5 DECEMBER 1899

N A T A L

Tugela R.

Pietermaritzburg

Durban

BULLER'S ARRIVAL
FROM CAPE TOWN
OCTOBER 1899

⇒ Boer forces
→ British forces

0 ——— 50 Miles

ORANGE FREE

STATE

Harrismith

Glencoe
Dundee

Elandslaagte

24 February 1900
Spionkop

5 January 1900
Vaalkrantz

Ladysmith

15 December 1899
Colenso

Tugela R.

Chieveley

0 10 20 Miles

Estcourt

N A T A L

BULLER'S THREE BATTLES
ON THE TUGELA

93

58. Louis Botha soon after taking over as Commandant-General.

Command, was made corps Commander-in-Chief. His appointment, which was supported by the Queen, represented the triumph of the home forces over the Indian Army and was well received by the press. Buller had had experience in Africa during the Ashanti War in 1873, the Kaffir War of 1879 and the First Boer War. He was said to have looked the part of a successful general. Appearances, however, were deceptive. Not only had he no experience of commanding large bodies of men, but when faced with difficult decision he went to pieces. Buller's instructions were explicit: he was to attack immediately from the Cape. Plans had already been drawn up, based on the most suitable route, along the railway line from De Aar to Bloemfontein. Although the line was in Boer hands, they did not hold it in strength, since most of the commandos were busy besieging Ladysmith and the other towns. Nevertheless, Buller did not carry out this plan.

Buller arrived in Cape Town on 31 October and was greeted by such a deluge of bad news that he became convinced that White was about to surrender. It is difficult to know where he got this idea. It certainly was not from General White himself. Leaving Lord Methuen, commander of the 1st Division, to advance along the prepared route from the western Cape, Buller set out for Natal. He shipped a large part of his force to Durban and moved up the railway line to Chieveley, where he camped. Ahead of him across a wide plain was the Tugela River, beyond that the town of Colenso, at the foot of a series of hills. On the high ground a few miles north was Ladysmith, surrounded by Boers. At that time the north of Natal formed a wedge between the Orange Free State in the west and the Transvaal across the Buffalo River to the east. The Boers had invaded northern Natal at its apex and on both sides of the triangle; the early battles had been fought in the middle of the territory, along the railway. Buller's battles were on the Tugela, at the base of the triangle.

As Buller began preparing his offensive, the Boer forces reorganized to meet the attack. Joubert was badly hurt in a riding accident, so Louis Botha was placed in command. Although he was younger than many of the other commandants, he was well liked by both the Transvaalers and the Free Staters, and everyone felt that he would bring a new sense of purpose to the war. There were few objections to the changes he instituted. He placed a line of commandos on the hills above the Tugela and waited for Buller to attack. It was an excellent defensive position, protected by a river and by rising ground. There was no easy way round. Between 15 December and 5 February Buller carried out a series of frontal attacks on the Boer positions, all of which he lost.

Meanwhile, with Buller still preparing to advance, Lord Methuen suffered two serious defeats in the Cape. After minor engagements at Belmont and Enslin, on 28 November he launched

an early-morning attack by Guards regiments on General Cronje's positions at Modder River. For the first time, the British encountered De la Rey's tactical innovations. Instead of setting up a defence line behind the natûral barrier of the river, he dug trenches a few yards ahead of it. His idea was to discourage the Boers from retreating when the troops approached by keeping the river behind his men. The Boers, hidden in the trenches, were instructed to hold their fire until the British troops were well within range. De la Rey prepared the flat ground in front of them like a stage set. The whole fire-zone was marked with painted stones and tin cans, so that the rifle-sights could be accurately adjusted for distance. Previously, when the Boers had been positioned on the tops of small hills, the angle of fire had meant that even accurate shooting could only account for one man per shot. In the Modder River

59. This historic photograph taken after the Battle of Modder River shows one of De la Rey's trenches and the plain across which the guards advanced. The river is behind the photographer.

60. Terrain typical of the Modder River area where the Guards were pinned down all day by relentless Boer rifle-fire.

battle the Boers were shooting from ground level and bullets tore through the ranks, often injuring more than one man. Within a few minutes the lines of advance were pinned to the ground. The slightest movement provided a target, and many soldiers were wounded in the buttocks or heels. The troops just lay there all day until the sun set, suffering most terribly from the heat and lack of water. It was impossible for stretcher-bearers to retrieve the wounded, who could be heard cursing and moaning throughout the long day. Some went mad, or stood up and died when they could bear it no longer. The worst torture was caused by ants disturbed by the artillery bombardment, which crawled all over the troops, biting any exposed flesh they could find. Scotsmen in kilts suffered most: as well as being bitten by ants, many had the skin burned off the backs of their legs by the sun.

After the battle, Cronje retreated to Magersfontein and set up a defence line in front of a row of low koppies. A long trench was dug, strengthened by barbed-wire fences. These were arranged so as to direct the advancing soldiers into a narrow zone where the most damage could be done by concentrated rifle fire. After a few days' rest, Lord Methuen decided on a surprise night attack. Late in the afternoon of 10 December a force consisting mainly of Scottish regiments, commanded by the famous General Archie Wauchope, set off towards the Boer position. After a difficult advance through rain the men ended up crowded together by the wire. As the first light came up the front ranks were devastated by a thunderous fusillade from the trench just ahead of them. Within minutes they had suffered heavy casualties. Wauchope was killed in the first fire; later his friends wrote that he had had a premonition of death. For the first time in modern history Scottish troops turned and ran. To this day the retreat is commemorated in the uniform of the Scottish regiments which took part, by circular cuts in the fronts of their spats.

Meanwhile, further to the east, another disastrous engagement had taken place. General Gatacre ('Back-breaker' to his troops) had been instructed by Buller to attack in the centre of the Cape line, while Methuen advanced on the left. On 9 December he set out on a night march to Stormberg Junction, an important connection on the railway line from East London to Bloemfontein. His plan was to carry out a surprise attack at dawn, but everything went wrong. The men were tired before starting, having been kept waiting for hours beforehand without food and water. They took a wrong turn in the dark and, instead of reaching the Boer line in a couple of hours, marched on and on until dawn. As soon as it became light they were spotted. Too tired to put up much resistance, they were routed by the Boers in a few minutes. Although there were less than 100 casualties, nearly 600 were captured.

It was now Buller's turn to run into trouble. On 15 December he advanced across the plain towards Colenso. The battle began with an artillery bombardment of the high ground, where Botha was thought to be waiting. Lyddite shells were used, and through a telescope Buller watched the hilltops being torn to pieces. However, Botha had adopted De la Rey's ideas and entrenched his commandos on both banks of the river, well ahead of their expected position, so that no one was killed by the exploding shells. The Boers held their fire until the troops were well within rifle range. Botha's plan had been to allow the main force to cross the bridge to Colenso, and then to attack from behind. Fortunately for the British, someone began shooting before they had crossed the river, otherwise the losses would have been much heavier. Nevertheless the attack ground to a halt before the main force was across. On the right, Colonel Long advanced his battery of twelve guns too close to the Boer positions, well within rifle range, and soon they ran out of ammunition. Within a few minutes the guns had to be abandoned because the crews were all dead or wounded. A number of officers volunteered to bring them back, and it was during one of these brave but unsuccessful attempts that Lord Roberts's son, Fred, was fatally wounded. Buller lost his nerve and ordered the withdrawal of the whole force. Further casualties were suffered during the retreat and the guns were ignominiously left behind for the Boers to collect, even though they could have been removed during the night.

The week of 10 to 17 December 1899, when the battles of Magersfontein, Stormberg and Colenso took place, is called 'Black Week'. In a few days the British Army, the 'Pride of the Empire', suffered a series of unprecedented catastrophes at the hands of a non-professional army. Nearly 3,000 men were killed or wounded and a whole battery of field-guns lost. In the nineteenth century there was no greater military ignominy than to abandon guns to the enemy. The worst humiliation occurred when Buller panicked and signalled White to surrender. Later he denied that he had sent the message.

In Britain there was a public outcry. On 18 December the government replaced Buller as Commander-in-Chief. Lord Roberts, who had been writing to anyone with influence in Whitehall about the way the war should be handled, was placed in command. He had retired from the Indian command three years previously and many people thought that he was too old for such a difficult post. Kitchener, the hero of the Sudan, who certainly had plenty of energy, was appointed his Chief of Staff. In addition the government called up the remaining reserves and ordered their dispatch with loads of equipment. They also set up new regiments such as the Mounted Yeomen and accepted substantial help from the Empire.

During his preparations Roberts instructed Methuen and Buller to take no further action. But Buller was not easy to stop. Like a cart careering down hill without brakes, he fought two more battles before finally shuddering to a halt. Moving his vast force west along the Tugela on 10 January, he entrusted the attack to General Warren, an ex-police officer. After days of procrastination Warren crossed the river and stormed the heights on its north bank during the night of the 22nd. When the sun rose and the Natal morning mist cleared, the troops found themselves on a central hill, Spionkop, surrounded on three sides by heavily defended ridges at an even higher level. Worse still, it turned out that in the dark they had failed to clear all the Boers from the hill.

The battle which followed was characterized by exceptional bravery on both sides; close hand-to-hand fighting alternated with devastating artillery bombardments. The officer in charge, Woodgate, was killed, and no orders or help came from Warren or Buller throughout the day. At one point Churchill (still a war correspondent) climbed the hill. He returned to Warren's headquarters and reported that the day would be lost unless reinforcements were immediately sent up. Warren did nothing. In the evening, after the loss of 1,200 men, the troops retreated, leaving the Boers in possession of the summit. It was the worst defeat suffered by a British army since the Crimea. In the morning the Boers took photographs of the British dead which were published throughout the world and caused uproar in England.

Here is an extract from a letter to a Mr Raphael about the death of his son Frederick:

> Dear Mr Raphael,
>
> With great sorrow and in heartfelt sympathy I write to announce to you the death of your son Frederick, killed in action on Spionkop hill on the morning of the 25th. Many brave and noble fellows fell that awful morning but not one of them is more regretted than your son.
>
> Two companies of his battalion were detached to take part with other troops in the attack on a high ridge – nay a precipitous mountain. The ridge was carried by assault after a toilsome night's work – all except the spur of the hill, unfortunately strongly held.
>
> The captain of your son's company was shot during the first assault – your son then bravely took command and some two hours after his captain's death, was himself instantly killed by shell fire in the head. He had been encouraging his men all morning by word and example, and is reported to have himself shot five of the enemy dead before his own noble death.
>
> Your dear son, all of him that is mortal, lies decently and reverently buried on that ill-fated ridge surrounded by comrades and friends.[20]

Even then Buller could not be stopped. Ignoring Roberts's order, on 5 February he attacked again further west at Vaalkranz. The battle went on for some days to little effect before Buller once again withdrew. By then Roberts was nearly ready to attack from the Cape, and the whole war changed direction.

ROBERTS'S MARCH TO PRETORIA

Roberts and Kitchener landed in Cape Town on the last day of December and immediately set about reorganizing the Cape command. Buller's method of slow advance was obviously useless against the Boers. For an attack to be successful it had to be part of a highly mobile campaign based on carefully planned outflanking manoeuvres. Roberts decided to launch the attack from the Cape, as the War Office had originally intended. Within hours the

61. Boer photographs taken on the morning after the Battle of Spionkop. The British trench has become a mass grave.

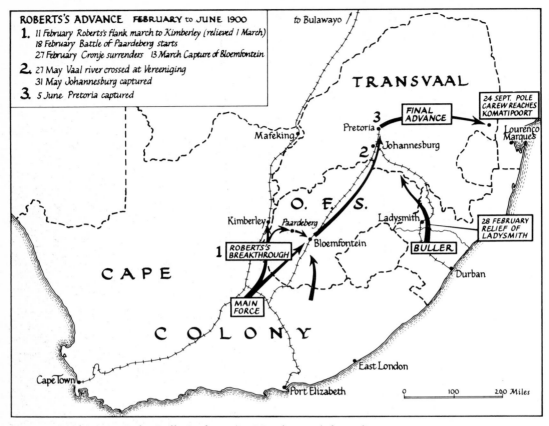

ROBERTS'S ADVANCE FEBRUARY to JUNE 1900

1. 11 February Roberts's flank march to Kimberley (relieved 1 March)
18 February Battle of Paardeberg starts
27 February Cronje surrenders 13 March Capture of Bloemfontein

2. 27 May Vaal river crossed at Vereeniging
31 May Johannesburg captured

3. 5 June Pretoria captured

regrouping began. Only Buller's force in Natal was left undis-
turbed. Every other unit was reassembled into a tactical force
designed for rapid movement. The changes affected the regiments
which Roberts had brought with him as well as those already in
service in South Africa. The aim was to get as many troops as
possible into the saddle, and it was no easy task. The army was
critically short of experienced cavalry. Most of the mounted regiments had been distributed among infantry battalions, to be
used mainly as scouts. These were hastily reformed into cavalry
regiments near the Modder River line, with General French in
command. They were to play a crucial role in the attack which
Roberts and Kitchener were planning. In addition, strenuous
efforts were made to build up as many regiments of mounted
infantry as possible. Officers of foot regiments were instructed to
raise at least one company of mounted men from soldiers who
could ride. In every unit men could be seen practising or learning
to ride, and within a few weeks the best had been formed into
two new brigades.

Even then Roberts's needs had not been met. A variety of new
regiments, with names such as Kitchener's or Roberts's Horse,

62. Roberts and Kitchener landing in
Cape Town.

were formed from colonial volunteers. Although many of these men were excellent riders and knew the country well, they had little military training and were not of much use in the initial advance, though their value increased progressively during the months that followed. However, most of the army could not be mounted. The limiting factor was the shortage of horses. Kitchener made strenuous efforts to make up the deficiency by cutting the number of horse-carts in the supply columns, and vast convoys of ox-wagons and mule carts were accumulated. It nevertheless became evident that most of the men were really going to march

63. Newly arrived troops receiving instruction in horsemanship.

to Pretoria. This was a time of great excitement for the troops, whose morale rose as soon as they recognized that an experienced hand was on the helm. They were eager to get going.

Meanwhile Buller had fought and lost the battle of Vaalkrantz. It seems to have been impossible for Roberts to stop him, and his force of more than 40,000 men was not included in the planned move. Roberts concentrated on the preparations in the Cape, where there had been little activity since the Battle of Magersfontein. However, in Methuen's front line this period had not been entirely without incident. Colonel Sir John Hall of the Coldstream Guards wrote:

On the first occasion on which the 2nd Battalion was on outpost duty after the retreat an unfortunate incident occurred which deprived it of the services of Lieut. H.A. Chandos-Pole-Gell. On the morning of the 15th December, while the guns were shelling Magersfontein Hill, Captain R.C.E. Skeffington-Smyth was informed by an artillery officer that a flag of truce was coming in about noon and that it was to be met by an officer in front of the entrenched outpost line. Shortly afterwards Lieut. Chandos-Pole-Gell, under the mistaken impression that he could perceive a white flag, borrowed a gunner's horse and rode out to meet it. He was unarmed and only carried with him a copy of the World newspaper, which he proposed to use as a flag of truce. After riding about fifteen hundred yards to the front, he was stopped by three Boers who, after hearing his explanation, took him into their lines. Here he was brought before Cronje, who accused him of spying and refused to believe his story. Lord Methuen, as soon as the matter was reported to him, wrote to the Boer general to assure him of the innocent nature of Lieut. Chandos-Pole-Gell's proceedings. But Cronje declined to be pacified, and merely returned a curt answer to the effect that he wished to have no further communication with Lord Methuen as long as the war lasted.[21]

On 11 January 1900 Roberts's attack began. After various diversionary movements General French's cavalry crossed the Reit River in a brilliant thrust which took them in a great arc round Cronje's position. No patrols were sent ahead, and French was lucky not to encounter Boer commandos in the open country. Behind the cavalry came the infantry. The only serious obstacle in the flat veld was the Modder River, but it was easily fordable during the dry summer months. However, the troops had to face the full rigour of a Free State summer. They set off early in the morning on a sixteen-mile march, but the going proved more difficult than was anticipated. It turned out to be one of the hottest days of the year. In one of the brigades half the men collapsed from heat exhaustion or sunstroke. Twenty-one died. Many of these were reservists who had just come up by train from Cape Town, having left the British winter behind only a few weeks earlier. Nevertheless, in spite of the difficulties the entire division had been reconstituted on the north bank of the river by the 14th.

64. The attack begins.

The next few days saw dramatic events. On the 15th, French swept aside with a classical cavalry charge the last commando blocking his entrance to Kimberley. That evening he rode into town to an excited welcome. On the 16th Roberts moved head-quarters to Jacobsdal. It was his intention to transfer the re-mainder of his force to Kimberley, but he received information that General Cronje's commandos were retreating eastwards with a large train of wagons. Scouting parties were sent in search of them, and General Kelly-Kenny's division found them on the banks of the Modder River at Paardeberg Drift. At midnight on the 16th French raced from Kimberley with three cavalry regi-ments to intercept them. The following morning he found the enormous Boer laager, which stretched for six miles on either side of the river, and attacked immediately. Cronje's commandos still had their families and all their baggage with them, and in spite of the entreaties of numerous commandants to let the fighting men escape before they were surrounded, he refused to leave the con-voy. Instead he ordered his troops to dig trenches and prepare to defend themselves.

Kitchener arrived on the 18th and took advantage of Roberts's absence with a cold to attack. He rode from unit to unit shouting to them to advance towards the trenches. The battle continued for two days, with Kitchener pushing in troops from all sides and keeping up an artillery bombardment. Casualties were heavy, particularly among the Canadians: the Boers might be trapped, but they were ready to fight. At one point, Kitchener suddenly ordered the Mounted Brigade to ride towards the trenches. Their officer, Colonel Hannay, realized the uselessness of such an attack, but it was impossible to refuse the order. Turning suddenly to a small group of his troops, he ordered a charge. Hannay was killed as soon as he got near the laager. His suicidal action was recognized for what it was – a brave attempt to save the bulk of his men.

Roberts arrived on the 19th and immediately broke off the attack. From the 19th to the 27th he carried out a continuous bombardment with little loss of men, and his siege gradually wore down the Boers. Although De Wet and others were able to break through, they could not convince Cronje to cut his losses and get out as much as he could. On the 27th, the anniversary of the Boer victory at Majuba Hill, Cronje surrendered. He was taken to Roberts's camp, where they had breakfast together – at different tables.

The following day Buller relieved Ladysmith. For the first time he attacked Botha's line in a professional way. Advance after advance was made at different points. Each successful thrust was immediately reinforced, and the Boers' resistance crumbled. Buller rode into Ladysmith at the head of his column. On 13 March Roberts entered Bloemfontein. The Free Staters had decided not to defend the town after an inconclusive action on the 7th at Poplars Grove – the first of many engagements in which British troops attacked retreating commandos. Neither side was able to sustain a prolonged fight: Roberts's army was tired, and short of horses and supplies, and the Boers seemed to have lost all heart. Before the battle Kruger had rushed to the Free State to meet Steyn. Everything was done to encourage the burghers – Kruger himself had come up to the front to strengthen their resolve – but when the firing started, De Wet could not hold them and they ran. Kruger was caught in the rout and the old President, in black suit and top hat, only just managed to gallop away in his horse-drawn Cape cart.

In Bloemfontein Roberts was now forced to rest his entire army. It was six weeks before he could resume the advance. Much of this time was needed to replenish stocks of horses and mules which had been badly depleted by the hard work and terrible summer conditions. So many horses had died on the march that General French was accused of being a better cavalry officer than

65. General Cronje after his
surrender at Paardeberg.

horse-master, but many had been in poor condition when they
arrived in South Africa and they had certainly not been bred for
work in the veld. Every effort was made to restock with the best
available mounts: they were going to be needed to get this army
of 50,000 men through the arid country ahead.

In Britain the six-week delay seemed excessive. It was even
feared that the overcrowded conditions in the town might lead to
riots when Australians, New Zealanders, Canadians, British irregulars and South Africans were forced together for more than a
month with nothing to do. It was one of the major surprises of
the war that they behaved well. The main problem was a typhoid
epidemic.

British colonial doctors had considerable experience in treating
tropical fevers, especially in India. During the nineteenth century
great strides had been made in understanding the cause and prevention of such diseases. At first typhoid (or enteric fever, as it
was often called) was confused with other tropical fevers, particularly typhus, a disease spread by ticks. The French, notably
Bretonneau in 1829, were the first to differentiate between the
two, and in the middle of the century Sir William Jenner published
a detailed analysis of the symptoms and signs of the different
fevers. During the next few years numerous accounts of various
outbreaks of typhoid appeared in the medical press. In his report
on an epidemic in 1856 William Budd pointed out that the illness
appeared to be spread by the contamination of drinking water
with sewage. The disease could also be spread in milk. Most
outbreaks in nineteenth-century Britain occurred in large towns.
For instance, there were epidemics in Blackburn in 1881, in
Worthing in 1893, and in Maidstone in 1897.

When Roberts's corps was being recruited in England, volunteers were examined by army doctors and many turned down.
The medical reports caused considerable controversy because the
general health of the population was shown to be so poor. Those
who succeeded in joining had a short intensive training and were
shipped out to the Cape in the first available transport. They were
then immediately moved up to the front by train, and within a
few weeks were marched into the heat of an Orange Free State
summer. Some died during the first few days from heat-stroke.
This was expected, and with their tropical experience, army
doctors were able to keep the fatalities to a minimum. The trouble
really began during the halts. Supplies of clean water could not
be obtained, and the men were forced to drink from any river in
the neighbourhood, however polluted. Men started coming down
with fever as soon as they reached Bloemfontein. The town's
water supply was poor and easily infected, but it is also probable
that the troops' resistance had been lowered by their heavy march

66. Roberts's troop stopping for refreshment.

67. Aftermath of the typhoid epidemic.

without adequate food. They succumbed with frightening rapidity, and a major epidemic developed.

In an age of antibiotics and intravenous fluid replacement it is difficult to understand the terrors and suffering an enteric epidemic then involved. Lynch wrote a vivid impression of the illness:

Hot, sweating, dusty and tired. With no inclination whatever to move out of camp ... everyone knew it was only the climate, the hard work, and sometimes the indifferent food ... but a day comes when the food is absolutely distasteful, when the appetite begins to go. A long day's ride on the veldt should leave one with a voracious appetite for dinner, but when one comes in and can taste nothing, and only just lies down dog-tired day after day, then he begins to think there is something wrong. The idea of going to the doctor is very distasteful, so he struggles on, hoping to work it off, until one day he comes very near a collapse, with head swimming and knees groggy and then some comrade makes the doctor have a look at him, and his temperature is perhaps 102 to 104 ...

A curious passive fight the patient settles down to, with a fatal little thermometer keeping score and marking the game – a sort of tug-of-war between doctor and Disease. The ground is marked in degrees from 98.4 to 106, the former being normal temperature, and the latter the point at which, as a rule, Disease wins the game ... At the very start Disease had pulled him nastily close to the line, and was still pulling him over, and his temperature was rising point by point. There are various methods of treatment – with him they fought it with a drug called phenacetin and to the lay mind a wonderful drug it appears ... No sooner was a 5-grain dose swallowed than the temperature stopped on its upper course, then, gradually, like a good Turkish bath, the pores of the skin opened, and a most complete and profuse perspiration ensued, which was allowed to go on for a couple of hours. Then with the bed and bed-clothes drenched, he lay weak, limp, and feeling like a squeezed sponge, but with a temperature that showed three degrees marked down towards his own line...

Deaths from typhoid are not simply caused by a high body temperature, but often result from complications. Lynch continues:

A sufferer farther down from time to time called aloud in agony from the terrible splitting pains in his head ... His room-mate on his right got delirious and refused all nourishment. He struggled violently even against the stimulants prescribed ... nurse would spend half an hour trying to get a little down. Then he had seen an extreme attempt to feed him one night. He was held while a tube was passed through the back of his nose and so down his throat, but no sooner as it was down than the strength of fever, like that of a maniac, proved too strong for his nurses; they could no longer hold him. There was a horrible struggle with choking coughs and dark blood flowing from his nostrils, and the brandy was spilt on his face and smarting in his eyes. He spent days dying, and more rapid and more feeble grew his pulse and many times the nurse said there was none perceptible, and then the life would flicker up again.[22]

At the height of the epidemic as many as fifty men a day became ill. By the beginning of April, when it began to burn itself out, almost 1,000 troops had died in Bloemfontein. This was only the first of a series of outbreaks. By the end of the war nearly 21,000 soldiers had died in South Africa. Less than 8,000 of these died of wounds; most of the rest succumbed to typhoid.

Meanwhile a battle had taken place a few miles from Bloemfontein which had given new heart to the Boers. In the Free State British troops had been moving freely around the veld without being attacked, and had soon linked up with Gatacre's forces from the eastern Cape. Many had visited the smaller towns and found the Union Jack flying. However, the Free State commandants held meetings with President Steyn and began to regroup. Christiaan de Wet rapidly emerged as the most forceful leader, and on 31 March he attacked a British column near the Bloemfontein waterworks. The dam lies about twenty miles from the town on the road to Thabanchu (Thaba 'Nchu is an African name meaning 'Black Mountain'). A column of supply wagons on its way to Bloemfontein was encamped nearby at a small railway station called Sannah's Post. It was being escorted by about 200 mounted infantry under General Broadwood, who commanded the garrison at Thabanchu. De Wet set a trap for the convoy with a commando of 1,600 men. While his brother Piet bombarded the camp from the north, De Wet hid in a dry river-bed in the convoy's path. Broadwood sent the wagons ahead to Bloemfontein while he faced the Boers who were firing at him. When the wagons appeared at the crossing they were captured and driven to a small farmhouse a few hundred yards away. In his book *The Three Years' War*, De Wet describes the incident:

Towards us, over the brow of the hill, came the waggons pell-mell, with a few carts moving rapidly in front ...

I was standing at the top of the drift with Commandants Fourie and Nel. I immediately ordered two of my adjutants to mount the carts and sit at the driver's side.

The other carts came one after the other into the drift, and I ordered them to follow close behind the first cart, at the same time warning the occupants that if they gave any signal to the enemy, they would be shot ...

So speedily did the carts follow each other that the English had no suspicion of what was occurring, and very shortly the soldiers began to pour into the drift in the greatest disorder. As soon as they reached the stream they were met by the cry 'Hands up!'

Directly they heard the words, a forest of hands rose in the air.

More troops quickly followed, and we had disarmed two hundred of them before they had time to know what was happening. The discipline among the burghers was fairly satisfactory until the disarming work began. If my men had only been able to think for themselves, they would have thrown the rifles on the bank as they came into their hands, and so

would have disarmed far more of the English than they succeeded in doing. But, as it was, the burghers kept on asking:

'Where shall I put this rifle, General? What have I to do with this horse?'

That the work should be delayed by this sort of thing sorely tried my hasty temper.[23]

Finally a British officer refused the order to put up his hands, turned and galloped back towards the camp. De Wet is said to have shot him with a rifle. This alerted Broadwood to the Boers

68. The 68-year-old Lord Roberts riding to Pretoria.

69. The Guards marching through the Transvaal.

behind him. Shooting started from all sides and Broadwood managed to extricate his remaining men to the east. In all, the Boers killed and wounded 170 men, took over 400 prisoners and got away with more than 80 supply wagons. The battle could be seen by an outpost on an isolated koppie a few miles away, but no help reached Broadwood from the town. It was a remarkable battle. Not only was it De Wet's best, but his success so soon after the loss of Bloemfontein convinced the Boers that it was possible to continue fighting in the veld even though the towns were in British hands. This was the first of many attacks by De Wet. Four days later he struck an isolated garrison at Dewetsdorp and captured nearly 600 regular soldiers. General Gatacre was in the vicinity but failed to give help. Roberts was furious and summarily sacked him.

At this time, however, De Wet's activities were not considered particularly important. By the end of April things had begun to improve in Bloemfontein. The epidemic was coming to an end; the men were rested; horses and equipment had been replenished. Roberts felt confident that he could tackle the 200 miles of veld which lay between him and the capital of the Transvaal. Perhaps remembering his dramatic march from Kabul to Kandahar in the Afghan War, twenty years previously, he gambled on rapid movement. It seemed likely that once both capitals were taken, all Boer resistance would collapse. Kruger was too old to take to the field as President Steyn had when Bloemfontein fell. However, if Roberts advanced too slowly, the Transvaal might be able to replenish its resources with gold from Johannesburg. European troops might even be brought in through Lourenço Marques, even though the British navy was still blockading the port. Holland and Germany were still making threatening noises.

Roberts's plan was to make a general movement of the whole army from Kimberley to Ladysmith. The only danger lay in leaving De Wet behind in the Free State. On 3 May the Transvaal offensive was launched. A vast army of 44,000 men, 11,000 horses, 120 guns and more than 2,500 wagons swept across the veld, pushing back and turning the flank of every commando which tried to oppose it. De la Rey cabled Botha in Natal that the 'English' crossing the plain were as numerous as locusts and could not be 'shot back'.[24]

On 16 May Mafeking was relieved by a 'flying column' from Rhodesia under Colonel Plumer and a column from the south commanded by Colonel Mahon of the Hussars. In the Free State, columns under French, Hamilton and Rundle pressed north. Roberts himself commanded a column in the centre. Although he was nearly seventy years of age he rode with the troops for more than six weeks.

On the 26th he crossed the Vaal River without difficulty and entered the Transvaal. Johannesburg surrendered without a fight on the 31st. The pro-Boer Irish politician Michael Davitt wrote, 'The English had at last planted their flag over the gold-reefed city of evil omen . . .'[25]

This time there was no delay in following through. A couple of days later Roberts pushed on the last few miles to Pretoria. Kruger had left on 19 May, after angry speeches in the Volksraad. On 5 June Roberts marched into the undefended city. Just after lunch he and his staff rode into the Central Square, and as the band of

70. Celebrations.

the Guards struck up the British National Anthem, a Union Jack
was hoisted on the Raadsaal. Roberts rode forward and called for
three cheers for the Queen. The whole Empire rejoiced.

5.   INTERVAL

The months between June 1900, when Roberts took Johannesburg, and January 1901, when he returned to England, were marked by a gradual deterioration of the situation in South Africa. This was not at first obvious. Roberts's brilliant dash to the Transvaal was proclaimed by the press as a campaign of military genius. It was compared favourably with his famous march in Afghanistan twenty years earlier. No one in Britain really thought that the capture of the Boer capitals could lead to anything less than a rapid surrender of the commandos. All that was needed was a mopping-up operation to deal with those Boers who had not given up their arms. If the commandants could be persuaded that the end was inevitable it would convince the rest that they had lost the war.

Roberts nearly succeeded. The Transvaalers were so demoralized when Pretoria fell that Botha called an armistice to consider whether they should continue fighting. When Kruger had left the capital, Botha had become President in everything but name. But the old man was still nominal leader; he moved the 'Presidency' eastwards and set up a sort of headquarters in a train near the border with Portuguese East Africa (or Mozambique). There was still a Transvaal government under Schalk Burgher, but it deferred to Botha for all major decisions. For the moment Botha and De la Rey remained in Pretoria to arrange for the city's surrender. It was particularly ironic that these men, who had spoken so strongly in the Volksraad against war before it began, should have been left to clear up the mess after Kruger's departure. Meanwhile Roberts's attention had been diverted back to the Free State which, although occupied by British troops, was causing trouble because of De Wet's repeated attacks on the railway.

After the surrender of the capital, the Transvaal leaders met just outside the city at a whisky distillery owned by Samuel Marks, a Johannesburg millionaire friend of Kruger's. They were there to decide whether to continue fighting. During the meeting a letter arrived from De Wet urging the Transvaalers to continue the war, and this swayed the balance. Both republican armies still had large stores of guns, ammunition and provisions; Smuts had managed to take nearly half a million pounds from the Transvaal treasury; and De Wet's recent success at Sannah's Post convinced them that it was still possible to remain in the field. His activities were best

71.

described by L.M. Phillipps, who served with Rimington during the 'De Wet hunts':

> De Wet is getting an immense reputation. The rapidity of his movements is extraordinary. He always has two or three of our columns after him; sometimes half-a-dozen. Among these he wings his way like a fowl of some different breed, a hawk among owls. Some amusement was caused by the report in orders the other day that De Wet had marched north pursued 'by various generals'; as if two or three, more or less, didn't matter, as indeed it didn't ... I think since the arrival of the main army he is the only man who has scored off us at all freely. Sannah's Post and Reddersburg came first; then, last May, came the capture of the 500 Yeomanry at Lindley; that was followed immediately by the surprise of the Heilbron convoy and all its escort; then came the capture of the Derbyshire Militia, and a few days later the taking of Roodeval with a train of mails and various details. Even when he had bolted out the other day between our legs, and was flying north with two or three cavalry brigades after him, he found time to snap up a hundred Welsh Fusiliers and break the line as he passed. He is, they say, extremely amusing, and keeps his men always in good temper with his jests; the other day after one of his many train captures, he sent a message to the base to say that 'he was sufficiently supplied with stores now, and would they kindly send up some remounts'.[26]

In strategic terms the Boers also had some reason for hope. Roberts's army was obviously unable to occupy the whole country, and assistance might be forthcoming from the Cape Afrikanders as well as from Europe, where the French and Russian governments were showing signs of a new interest. The Boers also remembered the way Gladstone had settled with them after Majuba. Lord Salisbury's government was not so conciliatory, but a general election loomed ahead. The Liberals might win and might be more amenable to negotiation. Botha broke off the discussions he had been secretly conducting with Roberts.

In Roberts's headquarters there was now considerable anxiety. The invading army had begun to melt away as the large force had to be broken up for various duties. But by the end of May the outlook had improved for the British: Buller began to move in Natal. He travelled slowly northwards during the next two months and in July linked up with Roberts, who now began to consolidate his hold on the Transvaal. On 12 June he attacked Botha at Diamond Hill, just outside Pretoria. The Boers retreated along the railway line towards Lourenço Marques and regrouped. Early in July Roberts attacked once again at Dalmanutha on the edge of the high veld. The battle continued for six days while Botha held out against overwhelming odds. It gave the burghers time to get away into the fever-ridden low veld. After a few weeks of difficult trekking, during which many contracted malaria, the stragglers regrouped in the northern Transvaal in areas out of British control. It was not until September that Roberts formally

72. Kruger landing in Marseilles after leaving South Africa.

annexed the Transvaal Republic for the Crown. Meanwhile in the Free State the British had another victory in July. Commandant Martin Prinsloo was chased into an area known as the Brandwater Basin which is surrounded by mountains; the passes were blocked and Prinsloo was captured with more than 4,000 men. In the Transvaal the advance also went well. The Mozambican border was reached in September, just after Kruger left South Africa for Europe. Even then the war did not end. Although many thousands of Boers had surrendered and were in prison camps, and others had given up the fight and gone home, Roberts had been unable to defeat either of the Boer armies.

Once again Roberts tried to get the Transvaalers to stop fighting. The two Boer armies had been separated by his advance and he hoped to widen the rift by negotiating with the Transvaalers, who were making a poor show of resistance compared with the Free Staters. On 2 September he threatened to destroy all farms near sabotaged railway lines. He also offered large annuities to Botha and De la Rey if they surrendered. The offer was refused.

However, there were many Boers who wanted to stop the war. The argument in De Wet's own family gives a dramatic illustration of what was happening in the commandos. Christiaan's younger brother Piet had been one of his most trusted commandants. Without him the surprise attack at Sannah's Post might not have succeeded. His subsequent position as one of the most despised men in the hierarchy of Afrikaans demons (a league-table based on cowardice, opposition to the war or working for the British) does not seem to be justified. After Sannah's Post his enthusiasm for the war gradually faded. He tried to discuss the subject with his brother, but Christiaan, busy with the day-to-day problems of the Free State, abruptly stopped him. Still he continued to brood on the cost of the fight to his country. On 19 May he made an offer to Roberts: he would surrender with 1,000 men if they would be allowed to remain in South Africa. He was told that surrender would have to be unconditional. Piet then resumed the campaign in the Free State, but on 26 July, during the first big hunt for his brother, he came into Kroonstaad with some of the men under his command. He refused to work for the British, but tried unsuccessfully to get others to lay down their arms. Christiaan, who was hard pressed at the time, must have been flabbergasted by the news. Early in 1901 Piet tried to explain his action:

Dear Brother,

I hear that you are so angry that you have decided to kill me, accusing me of high treason. May God not allow you the opportunity to shed more innocent blood! When I saw that we were beaten by the British I wrote to the President and requested him to consider terms of peace and rather to surrender than ruin the country and starve the people. I was afterwards with you for a month, and was then convinced that we had better lay down our arms, but I did my duty whenever we had an engagement. In the battle at Schietmekaar, with Prinsloo, I charged the guns when I was shamefully left in the lurch by Froneman, who fled. At last, convinced that the struggle was hopeless, I left with my staff, surrendered, and was sent to Durban.

The fact that you and Steyn were carrying on a guerilla warfare made me write to Lord Kitchener on December 11, requesting an opportunity to come to the Free State and persuade the men to lay down their arms as no Free State Government then existed against which I could commit treason.

Which is better for the Republics – to continue the struggle and run the risk of total ruin as a nation or to submit? Could we for a moment think of taking back the country if it were offered to us, with thousands of people to be supported by a government that has not a farthing and that has a debt of five or six millions, even if we received help from Europe? Do you think that any nation is so mad as to have thousands of men killed and spend millions of money, and then give us the Republics and the capital necessary to govern them? Put passionate feeling aside for a moment and use common sense, and you will then agree with me that

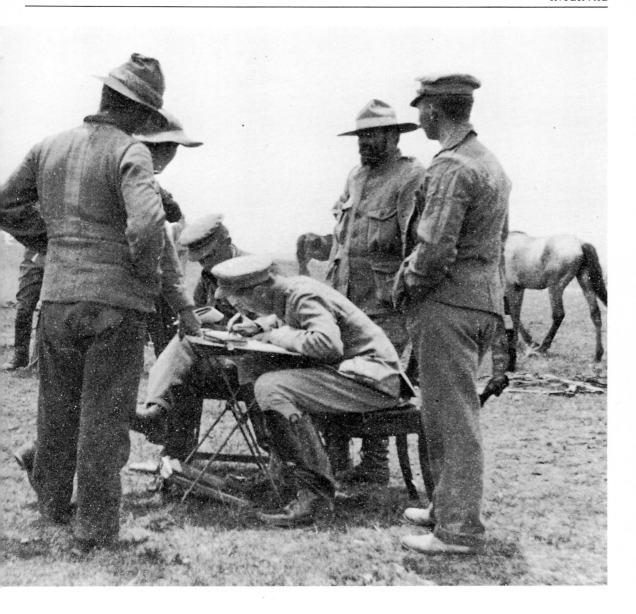

73. Boers signing the loyalty oath
after surrendering (1900).

74. Piet de Wet, Christiaan's brother.

the best thing for the people and the country is to give in, be loyal to the new government, and try to get responsible government. As soon as the finances allow of its being done we shall govern the country virtually ourselves, have our children properly educated and save the people as a nation. On the other hand, should the war continue a few months longer, the nation will become so poor, as a great portion already is, that they will be the working class in the country, and disappear as a nation in the future.

I have heard that you and the others accuse me of being paid by the English government for what I am doing. I can only answer, there is a

God. He will pass a righteous sentence. I have also heard that Lord Kitchener's offers and the attempts of myself and others are considered by you as signs of weakness on the part of the British. The British are convinced that they have conquered the land and its people, and consider the matter ended, and they only try to treat magnanimously those who are continuing the struggle in order to prevent unnecessary bloodshed.

Believe me when I tell you that no troops are being sent back to England, but that thousands are still coming to South Africa. If you consider the Free State you are not sensible, and do not act sensibly. Are you blind? Can you not see that you are being deceived by the Transvaal generals and burghers. What are they doing? They do not fight a tenth part as much as we do. The Transvaal is not ruined to the same extent as the Free State. The Transvaal generals are inclined to submit, and are only waiting to see what you are going to do. The moment you surrender, fall, or are captured they will surrender.[27]

De Wet flogged the man who brought the letter and sent him back with a message that he would shoot Piet 'like a dog' if he caught him.

The Boer fighters had every reason to keep going. The new Orange River colony had not been pacified. The British held only the big towns securely. As soon as troops moved out of a village, the Boers moved back in. The veld could only be said to be in British hands while they camped on it. In June De Wet still had about 9,000 men under arms in the north-east of the country. The area was very large, and Roberts decided that big troop concentrations were needed to deal with them. Three large columns moved through the territory looking for Boers and trying to drive them against columns which were camped along a line from Ficksburg to Senekal. But still De Wet's attacks continued. He hit isolated units wherever he found them, capturing convoys and sabotaging the railway whenever possible. About the time Roberts was pushing Botha towards the Mozambican border the Boer scout Danie Theron wrecked a train at Leeuwspruit. Kitchener was travelling on it and only escaped by jumping from a window, catching a horse and riding for his life to the nearest British camp.

This incident highlights the Boers' success in wrecking trains, which plagued Roberts and Kitchener throughout the war. No train was safe. At first they were derailed by setting off dynamite as the train passed. The attackers had to lie next to the line to light the fuse. This was highly dangerous, and the Boers subsequently developed a safer method of stopping trains without injuring passengers or damaging the supplies they needed. Old Martini-Henry rifles (for which there was no ammunition) were prepared by sawing off the butt behind the breech and removing the barrel a few inches in front of it. The trigger-guard was then removed and the breech opened. They inserted a cartridge without a bullet in the breech and placed a dynamite cartridge in the shortened barrel. Stones were then removed under the rail to make a hole, which was packed with dynamite. The mutilated breech of the rifle was then placed upside-down on top of the dynamite with the trigger just touching the rail. When a train passed, its weight made the rail sag and set off the trigger.

During this period the commandos were broken up into smaller units for specific tasks. When bigger engagements were planned it was no problem to assemble much larger forces with great speed. Between attacks, all units concentrated on cutting the railway. Nearly every week they disrupted Roberts's vital line of communication with Cape Town. For the first time the word 'commando' began to take on the connotations it had in the Second World War as a small, highly trained unit able to carry out surprise attacks far from its own lines.

For this type of warfare to be successful, military intelligence and communications had to be first class. Here the Boers held the ace. Not only could they expect a constant flow of information from sympathizers and spies all over the country, but they had an expert intelligence unit: Danie Theron's *Verkenners*, or scouts. Theron built up a highly trained force of more than eighty men

75. 'De Wet – his mark'.

76. Smaller commando units: detachment of burghers at Norval's Pont (1900).

who had been carefully chosen for their knowledge of the country and their scouting ability. Many were not Boers: at various times the unit was said to contain men from Holland, France, Germany, Russia, Ireland, Bulgaria, Turkey, Greece and Algeria.

Theron was a charismatic leader. Born in the Cape, he had practised as a lawyer in Krugersdorp before the war. Although his family was of Scottish extraction, he became a Boer hero during this period when he physically attacked the editor of the Johannesburg *Star*, a newspaper with pronounced Uitlander sympathies which had been conducting a brisk anti-Kruger campaign. He was arrested and convicted of criminal assault, but the fine was immediately paid by Boers in the court. He also took part in the commando which captured Jameson and his raiders. A month before the war Joubert appointed him commander of the Bicycle Dispatch Riders. The bicyclists served with distinction in Natal under Joubert and later under Botha. They worked not only as

77. The Boer scout, Danie Theron.

messengers but as reconnoitring parties for the commandos, and were often chosen for the most difficult tasks. Early in 1900 Theron was sent to join De Wet's commando in the Free State. He arrived just in time to take messages through the British lines to Cronje, who was surrounded at Paardeberg.

During the fighting which followed Roberts's advance the scouting activities of Theron and his men became a major element of De Wet's success. So much has been written about their exploits that Theron has become part of Afrikaans folklore. The tales tell of English-speaking guides who appear from nowhere, offer help to British units and disappear when these are unexpectedly ambushed. Even his death has a legendary quality. Early in September 1900, while trying to cut the main water supply to Johannesburg, he was attacked by a force under General Hart and driven back to some koppies near his home town. The story is that he had held off the surrounding troops for so long by the accuracy and volume of his rifle-fire that when it stopped the British were astounded to find only one dead body on the hill.

Boer women formed another important part of the communications network. The majority supported the war and gave as much help as they could. Many acted as couriers and spies for the Boers. An interesting account of this aspect of the war was written by Johanna Brandt of Johannesburg (see n. 44). She describes the way Boer women set up a secret communication system and managed to send letters to sympathizers in Europe and America, bypassing the strict military censorship. An important aspect of their work was to inform the commandos of Boers working for the British.

For their part the British relied on the telegraph system for communication. It was of little use to the Boers, who were always on the move, and in any case the British held all telegraph stations. On the other hand lines were constantly being tapped and could easily be cut at crucial moments when a coordinated attack was planned. Philip Pienaar, a Boer telegraphist, writes:

We two rode on until almost on top of the hill overlooking Heilbron, where we dismounted. Drawing the horses behind a low stone wall, we attached the instrument to the line. I listened. There were no fewer than five different vibrators calling each other, some strong and clear, others sounding weak and far, like 'horns of Elfland faintly blowing'. Presently, the disputed signals died away, and one musical note alone took up the strain.

Never was a lover more absorbed in the thrilling sound of his divinity's voice than I on the notes of that vibrator, seemingly wailing from the bowels of the earth.

Nor was my attention unrewarded.

'From Chief-of-Staff, Heuningspruit,' came the words, 'to General Hamilton, Heilbron.' Then followed orders. How Hamilton was to march from Heilbron; how Broadwood was to move from Ventersberg, the entire plan of campaign for the next four weeks![28]

It did not take long for the British commanders to become aware of the danger of telegraphic communication. But a complete ban on its use would have imposed insuperable difficulties on the army's chain of command. Roberts and Kitchener were forced to use codes.

As the months passed after the capture of Pretoria it became increasingly difficult to convince the British public that the war had ended. Gradually the newspaper reports began to take on a different tone: more effort was required to catch the guerillas; men and supplies were needed in increasing numbers. There was outspoken criticism in the press of the way the army was handling the situation. A mood of optimism still prevailed in political speeches, but throughout Britain organized groups began arguing that the war should be stopped on moral and political grounds. A similar situation was not seen again in any country fighting a war until Vietnam.

In many ways there are close parallels between the Boer War and the fighting in Vietnam. In both wars the governments of the strongest imperial powers of the age fought with overwhelming force against much smaller citizen armies. In both wars, as the fighting dragged on and on, people at home began losing their moral certainty about the fight. In Britain there had been considerable opposition to the war even before it began. It came in the main from members of the Liberal Party, which was in a state of disarray after Gladstone's retirement. Opposition to the Unionists gained momentum during the arguments which followed the Jameson Raid. It was stressed that Kruger was 75 years of age and that his political opposition had more liberal ideas. Joubert had been his likely successor and he spoke of conciliation. Many Liberals felt that the Unionist government had shown complicity with Rhodes, but its position was generally reinforced by the emotional jingoism accompanying Queen Victoria's Diamond Jubilee. Liberal politicians continued to voice their doubts about the Tory government's South African policy, but their arguments had little effect.

Even when the war started and the country was swept with patriotism, members of the Liberal Party continued to protest. Some of this opposition was purely expedient (the Party was trying to rally support), but there was also a moral and religious element. Sir Edward Clarke, who had been Solicitor-General to the Conservative government, was made to resign his parliamentary seat because he called the war unjust and unnecessary. The Liberal politician John Morley made speeches all over the country accusing the government of recklessness and lack of understanding. In the latter stages of the war he urged that the blacks should be fairly treated in the final settlement. These were just two voices among many.

Many of the anti-war faction suffered considerably for speaking out against it. On one occasion the young Lloyd George was nearly killed by a Birmingham crowd when he tried to address a meeting. He only just escaped from the hall under police protection. It did not stop his protests and he continued to make anti-war speeches all over the country. It was not easy to get a hearing in the Conservative newspapers. The *Morning Leader* and the *Star* were vigorously pro-Boer, but most of the Liberal papers eventually supported the Tory position. In the end the *Manchester Guardian* became the most important opposition newspaper.

An interesting difference between the situation in Britain at this time and America's experience during the Vietnam war was that university students, teachers and intellectuals were solidly against their country's foes. When politicians such as Morley or Campbell-Bannerman spoke in Oxford or Cambridge they could not even fill a hall with undergraduates. For the most part the Church was also on the side of the war party.

A number of organizations sprang up specifically to put the case against the war. The 'Transvaal Committee' was formed before the war by the 'Liberal Forwards' group whose aim was to prevent hostilities. The Labour Party was not yet very powerful, but its National Council also protested to the government. Some of the committees had no formal links with a political party. A Stop the War Committee was established at a conference of the Friends of Peace in January 1900, and issued pamphlets denouncing the fighting. The manifesto of a South African Conciliation Committee was given to the press on 15 January 1900 and it too put out political propaganda.

In mid 1900, heated arguments took place in the press and at public meetings about restrictions on freedom of speech in Britain. The pro-Boers were not given a fair hearing in the Parliament and were badly treated by the general public every time a meeting was held. The controversy continued in and out of the House during the remainder of the war. It reached a crescendo during Roberts's last months as commander, with the country approaching a general election. On 25 July 1900, Lloyd George said in the House of Commons, 'A war of annexation against a proud people must be a war of extermination, and that is unfortunately what it seems we are now committing ourselves to – burning homesteads and turning women and children out of their homes.' He warned the House that the government was using the war for electioneering.

The outbreak of the Boxer Rebellion in China temporarily diverted public attention from Africa and caused the Tories to delay the election. However, in September Lord Salisbury went to the country in what became known as the 'Khaki Election'. He fought the campaign from an overwhelming position of strength, convincing the electorate that the war was about to finish. The press

reported that Roberts was so certain of imminent success that he wanted to return to Britain. The opposition of a few untamed guerillas was not seen as a problem: they could be dealt with by a minor mopping-up campaign. Pro-Boers in the Liberal Party could find no support for their cause. Their campaign now concentrated mainly on the treatment of 'Cape rebels', Afrikander British citizens who were beginning to join the Boer forces. They were considered traitors by the British government and could be executed.

It was Joseph Chamberlain who had put pressure on Salisbury to go to the country. The Liberals spoke of 'Chamberlain's war and Chamberlain's election', and when the campaign started, Chamberlain was the dominating personality. He travelled everywhere, rushing from town to town making speeches, and sent out streams of telegrams and messages in support of other candidates. He even went to support young Winston Churchill at a meeting in Oldham. Churchill was the hero of imperialism; Lloyd George became its demon. At first the Welshman was attacked by enraged crowds whenever he spoke, but as election day approached he had begun to move crowds with his oratory. As with Churchill, the war set the pattern for his future sucess.

78. Lapel buttons from the 'Khaki Election' (1900): (*clockwise*) Alfred Milner, Joseph Chamberlain, Lord Salisbury, Cecil Rhodes.

After six weeks of frenzied activity the country went to the polls. The Unionists won outright, with 402 members returned to Parliament against 186 Liberals. Although this was only an increase of three seats, the Liberals had been soundly defeated. For the moment the anti-war policy was discredited in most parts of Britain.

In the aftermath of the election it really did seem as if the war was about to end. Roberts was soon to come home. Buller's field force in Natal was broken up and in October he returned to England. On the 19th Kruger sailed for Holland. Later that month the City Imperial Volunteers returned to London to be greeted by enormous crowds. Everyone felt that the final mopping up was a police action rather than a military campaign. One of Roberts's last acts was to organize a South African Constabulary. He put Baden-Powell in command and send him to England to raise recruits.

Roberts himself did not leave the country until the end of November, having been delayed by the illness of his daughter and by a fall from a horse which forced him to keep one arm in a sling. He returned to a delighted and thankful country which showed its appreciation by granting him £100,000 and making him a lord. Poor old Queen Victoria insisted on seeing him a few days before her death. Both Roberts and Buller received tumultuous ovations wherever they went. Not since Wellington's day had Britain experienced such scenes of military adulation, which were compared to victory marches in the heyday of Imperial Rome. Through it all Roberts protested that he had done very little and gave all the credit to his troops. Knowing the situation in Africa, he must have found it an embarrassing time.

After the election the anti-war parties took stock and began to campaign again. Protests were now aimed at specific points of the government's policy and at the harshness of Kitchener's methods. Gone were the pious declamations; now there were reasoned speeches from Liberal politicians, carefully argued newspaper articles and factual pamphlets put out by anti-war committees. They began to be directed increasingly against Kitchener's policy of clearing the land and burning the farms, which had begun in earnest. The displaced families were put in concentration camps, and by June 1901 the reports of Emily Hobhouse, a young Englishwoman who had visited the camps, were being widely discussed in serious papers and journals and had caused a wave of consternation throughout the country. In increasing numbers, serious people began to speak out publicly against the programme of destruction.

Women's organizations were at the forefront of the campaign. For the first time in British history a broad spectrum of women became politically active, and their experience helped to form a basis for the later growth of the women's suffrage movement, which had yet to develop popular appeal. In some cases this orientation to current events and general policy rather than to issues specific to women resulted from a conscious political decision. In May 1901 the *Manchester Guardian* reported on a meeting of the Women's Liberal Federation at which it was decided to concentrate for the time being on attacking the conduct of the war rather than on discussion of women's suffrage.

In June the Women's Branch of the South African Conciliation Committee held a meeting in the Queen's Hall in London. Men were excluded, but a Mr Courtney managed to get in and reported the proceedings in the papers. The meeting, attended by women from all over Britain, passed a number of resolutions which were definitely political. They condemned the 'unhappy' war, which, they said, was mainly due to the government's bad policy. It had already cost, in killed, wounded and missing, over 20,000 brave soldiers; what was more, it had cost millions of pounds from the savings and toil of the British people. The two small states with which Britain was at war were being utterly ruined. The women protested that the government and its supporters were restricting all freedom of speech and any criticism of government policy. They warned against any settlement which involved the breaking up of the Republics, whose inhabitants, 'allied to us in blood and religion, cling as passionately to their separate nationality and flag as we in this country do to ours'. The meeting ended with a resolution expressing sympathy with the women of the Transvaal and Orange Free State and begging them to remember 'that thousands of English women are filled with profound sorrow at the thought of their sufferings, and with deep regret for the actions of their own Government'.[29] To any previous generation this would have been treason.

By the end of the year even the Establishment papers such as *The Times* had published letters expressing anti-war sentiments. Leading lights of the Liberal Party's anti-war faction such as Campbell-Bannerman, Lloyd George and John Morley were listened to with a new interest. The protesters gave the Boers an additional reason to continue fighting, of this there is no doubt. But the pro-Boer campaign was never anything more than a minority movement in Britain. The majority of ordinary people, supported by the Anglican Church and the army, remained stoutly behind the imperialist policies of the Unionists. Even in Wales, which (particularly in Welsh-speaking areas) was more strongly pro-Boer than any other part of Britain, this was a minority opinion. Only the Irish wanted the Boers to win; in Britain even the pro-Boers were for conciliation. But although the protesters' actions had little effect on the outcome of the war or on the way it was conducted, a climate of opinion was produced which led, when the war ended, to an early recognition of the Boer military leaders as political representatives of their nation. In less than eight years Botha was Prime Minister of the Union of South Africa.

6. KITCHENER TAKES OVER

For Kitchener, the war in South Africa must have been a very difficult time. He had set his mind on becoming Viceroy of India and had been conniving with friends in Whitehall to get the post of Commander-in-Chief of the Indian Army as a stepping-stone. Unfortunately for him the incumbent, Lockhart, died unexpectedly in March 1900, during the advance to Pretoria, when it was quite impossible for Kitchener to leave Africa. Sir William Palmer was posted to India as acting C.-in-C., which left Kitchener with some hope for the future. He wrote to Brodrick, who had become Secretary of State for War after the October election, about the possibility of obtaining the Indian appointment after the Boers were defeated. The reply was a severe disappointment. There was strong pressure in the Cabinet to bring him back to England to reorganize the War Office. As with so many previous wars, a disastrous campaign was having its effects in Whitehall. It was a position he dreaded, for he considered himself, with some justification, unequal to a task which would involve such delicate and involved political machinations. Once more he appealed to friends with Cabinet influence, and in March he was delighted to receive a cable from Brodrick saying that Palmer's appointment was only for a year, and that after Kitchener had given assistance in London the Indian post would be vacant. One can imagine his frustration during Roberts's last months, as he saw the old man losing control of the situation. On Roberts's departure Kitchener stepped confidently into the command, bringing with him a new sense of urgency.

In fact he inherited a situation which seemed to be worsening on every side. De Wet, Botha and De la Rey were as active as ever; moreover the events of the previous six months had demonstrated how difficult it was even to come to grips with them. Each Boer leader was a virtual prince of his own region – De Wet in the Free State, Botha in the eastern Transvaal and De la Rey in the western Transvaal. In spite of the density of British troops on the ground, there were still excellent communications between the three forces. However, there were tensions in the Boer camp – concerted action would have been easier if De Wet had not been so suspicious of Louis Botha – but De la Rey, as the acknowledged elder statesman, was able to keep the peace. Within their own territories they retained right to the end the ability to organize operations involving cooperation by several commandos. A dossier of Botha's papers captured at this time shows that when he planned an important attack he would instruct commandos to break railway lines simultaneously all over the country in order to prevent British troops being transported to the area of the action. This point needs to be stressed because most British sources contended that it was purely a guerilla war, with individual 'terrorists' acting however and wherever they could.

Towards the end of 1900, soon after the death in Pretoria of Kruger's wife, Botha and Smuts met Steyn and De Wet at Cyferfontein to talk about the future. There was much to discuss. All of them felt that in tactical terms the fight could be continued almost indefinitely, despite the difficulty in obtaining supplies. The policy of removing Boer families from their farms was looked on as a major factor in allowing the war to continue, rather than a source of pressure on the men to surrender. It meant that the burghers no longer had to worry about their wives and children, who were being housed and fed by the British. As arms wore out and ammunition was used up, the Boers began to rely increasingly on captured British equipment. Bullets were easy to obtain: one only had to follow a column to find hundreds lying where they had been dropped, unused on the veld. Even rifles were readily available. Small units which became separated from a column at night were easy prey, and there were supply depots all over the country to pounce on when stores ran really low. It amused the Boers to think that they were living off the British taxpayer.

Strategic considerations were more of a worry. Once again the question was raised of whether anything could be gained by continuing the war. There were many things against going on: the election in Britain had shown that an increased majority of the electorate supported government policy; the pro-Boers in the Liberal Party had been soundly defeated; no help could be expected from Europe. Germany, France and Holland had let the Boers down badly. Even the Kaiser was now saying that he had been forced by his uncle the Imperial Chancellor into sending his famous telegram about the Jameson Raid.

Kitchener, however, was in no position to deal a decisive blow. Although he had inherited 210,000 troops in the Free State and the Transvaal commands, less than 150,000 could be relied on for active fighting duty. A further 50,000 were required to guard the lines of communication and at any time a further 20,000 were out of action because of ill-health or were on leave. He also found that there was a constant loss of trained regulars as they came to the end of their enlistment contracts. Their places were gradually taken by South African, Australian and New Zealand colonials who had little military experience, or by volunteers from Britain with almost no practical training. The Boers who were still fighting were now veterans with proven ability and tenacity. Roberts had already found that the army was not big enough for the job of 'pacification'. Although Kitchener asked for and got an increasing amount of modern equipment, the government appeared to be losing interest in the South African war as the situation in China became more and more worrying. It was in no mood to send more troops.

In February 1901 Kitchener made contact with Botha through his wife, who was living in Pretoria. Once again he offered to meet the Boer leaders to negotiate a peace. Botha was keen to meet him, but De Wet, still strongly under the influence of President Steyn's hard-line views, refused to take part. Botha did meet Kitchener at Middelburg on the last day of February. They got on well and had extensive discussions, but there were differences which could not be resolved. The meeting did, however, have important consequences after the war because it led to De Wet becoming suspicious of Botha's motives, an opinion he retained for the rest of his life.

For the moment the fighting went on. It was a good time for the Boers, with all three commanders active in their respective areas. De la Rey's 'kingdom' in the Magaliesburg region had few railways and roads, which made it more difficult for British columns to penetrate than Botha's eastern Transvaal or De Wet's area in the Free State. During the quiet period while Roberts had been concentrating on attacking De Wet and Botha, De la Rey had begun to build up his commandos. Roberts had taken action against him on a number of occasions with limited success, and Kitchener also found it difficult to deal with him, preferring to concentrate on the other two forces. The three Boer commanders had very distinct styles of leadership. Botha was charming and had an easy manner with his men; De Wet preferred to be in total control; De la Rey built up a strong group of commandants who could be relied on to take autonomous action, the best of whom were Kemp, Beyers, Lemmer and Smuts. Either in concert or separately, their commandos roamed the veld at will, attacking convoys and garrisons right up to the edge of Pretoria. De la Rey was supersititious. He was often visited by a *siener* (prophet) named van Rensberg, whose relationship with De la Rey was a curious one. He would appear suddenly, proclaiming his occult powers, and tell of mystical dreams which he interpreted as predicting the collapse of the enemy. De la Rey, who led many attacks in person, was said to consult him before every battle. On one occasion De la Rey captured a convoy near Pretoria which was loaded with provisions. He took as much ammunition, food and supplies as his men could carry, but gave all the alcohol (which he would not allow to his burghers) to the captured soldiers. They crowded round his wagon singing, 'For he's a jolly good fellow'.

De la Rey was very good at encouraging his junior officers. Smuts was particularly useful to him, proving to be as efficient a commandant as he was an administrator. De la Rey often sent him off to settle disputes among the burghers, a task which the young man compared with cleaning the Augean stables. Smuts liked commando life and was already thinking of leading an invasion into the Cape. It was a time of contemplation for him and he wrote a good deal, even sending articles about the farm-burning to magazines in Europe. Beyers was another young commandant who proved his worth; in particular he showed great courage and ingenuity in attacking British columns.

In spite of the continuing activity of British columns in all regions, the Boers now decided on a daring initiative. The war had begun with the Boers invading British territory, but Roberts had driven them back into the remoter parts of their republics. As 1900 drew to a close they determined to invade the Cape Colony and Natal for a second time. There was going to be no outside help, and it was becoming obvious that the British did not easily abandon a fight, despite what had happened in 1881. One last hope of assistance remained – from the Afrikander colonials in the Cape.

It had been a major disappointment to most Boers that Cape Afrikanders as a whole had sat on the sidelines when the war started. Many had, however, joined in as individuals: although British citizens, nearly 10,000 of these colonists had enlisted in the commandos. During Roberts's advance some had been captured, of whom the majority had been tried and convicted of 'treasonable activities'. A few had been jailed, most fined and sent home. The authorities probably thought that harsh sentences would do more harm than good in the Cape. When the Boers invaded for a second time the British government's reaction was different. 'Rebels' who were caught were sometimes executed. Between December 1901 and June 1902, more than 700 sentences were passed on rebels in the Cape Colony alone under the martial law imposed by Kitchener. Many of these were death sentences, although in most cases they were not carried out.

A number of other captured Boers were sentenced for 'criminal' acts. The best known of these was Commandant Gideon Scheepers of the Free State, who was captured in October 1901 when he was unable to get away from a pursuing column while suffering from appendicitis. In December he was tried at Graaff Reinet on charges of murder, arson, train-wrecking and ill-treatment of the wounded. He was found guilty and sentenced to death. On 18 January he was tied to a chair and shot. His body was buried in an unmarked grave, and after the war his parents spent years looking for it. The Afrikaans writer Meintjies tells of a tradition that his ghost still haunts the area.

The trials had little effect. The anti-war campaign had started up again in Britain, and the Cape Afrikanders showed signs of taking a more active part in the war. The commandos held secret meetings with messengers from the pro-Boers in the Cape. It was decided that if commandos could establish themselves in the central part of the Cape Colony, there was a fair chance that they would be augmented by local recruits. At the very least an invasion into the Cape and Natal would force Kitchener to transfer large numbers of troops from the Boer homelands, thus relieving the constant pressure on the commandos there. A new major offensive was agreed upon. The gold mines in Johannesburg would be blown up after two forces of 5,000 men each under De la Rey and Botha had been sent in. Botha would then re-invade Natal while De Wet entered the Cape Colony. If they were successful and Cape Afrikanders came to their aid, enabling them to capture the deep-sea ports and keep out British reinforcements, there was even a chance that the whole British army would collapse.

Fortunately for Britain the Boers failed to achieve their major objectives. The plan to destroy the Reef mines never got off the ground, and both De Wet and Botha were prevented from invading British territory. Botha was harried at every point and never got across the Natal border; De Wet succeeded in entering the Cape, but was forced to retreat back into the Free State after being chased for weeks by a massive drive known as the 'Second De Wet Hunt'. Nevertheless, by the first week of January 1901, small units of Boers under dynamic commandants such as Hertzog (who subsequently founded the National Party in opposition to Botha), Wessels, Fouche, George Brand, Kritzinger, Malan, Scheepers and Pretorius had begun operating in the Cape to the dismay of the authorities. Their activities continued with varying success for the remainder of the war, culminating in General Smuts's famous and arduous campaign. This took him right across the colony to the outskirts of Port Elizabeth and finally, after skirting Cape Town, to the little mining town of O'kiep in the northwestern Cape, where his force was still active when the war ended.

The start of these invasions coincided with Roberts's triumphant return to England. It was left to Kitchener to deal with the realities in Africa.

7.   TWENTIETH-CENTURY WAR

Roberts's final instructions had been to reduce the size of the columns, for speed, and to station garrisons at supply depots and along the lines of communication. Between the garrisons, patrols moved continuously. He believed that the war could only be ended by disarming every inhabitant of the old Republics.

The policy seemed reasonable to Kitchener. He must have felt that his energy would make up for previous failures; not for nothing was he known as 'the Machine'. To achieve efficiency, he set about reorganizing his forces. His first act was to abolish divisional action; large units were broken up and refashioned into groups of brigades. He had 38 such brigades, at least 26 of which were led by young officers with local or temporary rank indicating that they had been promoted as the result of proven practical ability. He divided the brigades into groups under divisional generals and set about deploying them in regions where the Boers were especially active, so that their time would not be wasted. The territory was divided into squares, each covered by a group of brigades; each unit was allocated a clear task and a well-defined area in which to act: chessboard war had begun.

Units were now living semi-permanently in each district and were encouraged to get to know their assigned territory as well as the local commando. It was an approach which proved more and more useful as regional knowledge increased. Regionalization also helped the mobile columns. Well-guarded provision camps were established near the railway lines, so that columns on the move would never be far from help if attacked and could replenish their horses and supplies efficiently and safely. The task of reorganization was enormous: for a time Kitchener seemed to be everywhere, handing out new commands to any officer he chanced to meet, making instant decisions about apparently trivial matters, moving units all over the place. He was never one to delegate.

Next Kitchener directed attention to the columns, which still moved too slowly. It was imperative that more troops should be mounted. The problem was to get enough horses. It became a constant battle. Some of the diarists record nights spent 'commandeering' horses wherever they could be found, mostly from other British units in the neighbourhood. There were even instances of animals being painted to disguise them from their real owners when the sun rose. For the army bureaucracy, the value of horses

79. In a fixed garrison.

became an obsession, as Corporal Ross of the Sussex Imperial Yeomanry discovered to his cost:

I told the latter that my horse was done, and the noble steed bore out my statement by collapsing under me as I spoke. The officer advised me to wait for the main body and lead my horse on after them, which I did, dragging him along for about a dozen weary miles, till I reached the camp at dark, just in time to participate in a lovely out-lying picket. The next morning, having reported the case to the sergeant-major, he told me to lead the horse from the camp with the convoy, and instructed the farrier-sergeant to shoot him a little way out. So, having put my saddle on our wagon and asked the farrier if he had been told about the shoot-ing, I proceeded to drag the poor beggar along. After toiling forward for some considerable distance, I looked around for the man whose duty it was to shoot him, but could see him nowhere. So on I pushed, inquiring of everybody, 'Where is the Farrier-Sergeant?' I lagged behind for him, and then toiled perspiring and ankle deep in dust, ahead for him, but found him not. Even during the mid-day halt I could not find him, and as the beast had fallen once, I was getting sick of it. Everybody I accosted

80. Remount camp.

advised me to shoot the brute myself, the same as the other fellows did in most of the Colonial corps, so at length ... giving up all hope of being relieved of my burden by the Farrier-Sergeant, who somewhere was ambling along comfortably on a good horse – having again had the sorry steed fall – I led him aside from the track of the convoy and ended his South African career with my revolver. Alas, Bête Noire! Had we but understood one another better the parting would have been a sad one. The case being otherwise, I felt, it must be admitted, no regret whatever. And now the interesting part of the episode begins. Hearing my shots (I am sorry to say I fired more than once in accomplishing my fell deed) the Farrier-Sergeant galloped up.

'Who gave you permission to shoot this horse?'

'Nobody; I couldn't find you, and couldn't lug the brute any further.'

'I shall report you.'

'I don't care.' Then followed high words, involving bitter personalities, and we parted.

... the Regimental Sergeant-Major came up and told me that he must put me under arrest for shooting my horse without permission, destroying Government property ... There was none of the pomp about the affair

81.

which I should have liked to see ... Our Sergeant-Major, without even removing his pipe, said, 'Ross, you are a prisoner.' ... A few days later, I was brought before the beak ... The Farrier-Sergeant told the requisite number of lies. I denied them, but of course admitted shooting the beggar. Dirty, unwashed, unkempt, unshaven, ragged wretch that I looked, I dare say on a charge of double murder, bigamy and suicide, I should have fared ill. The Captain gave me what I suppose was a severe reprimand, told me that probably in Pretoria I should have to pay something and said he would have to take away my stripe, so down it went, 'reduced to the ranks'.

'Salute! Right turn, etc.' Thus did your humble servant lose the Field Marshal's baton which he had so long been carrying in his haversack.[30]

The whole country was littered with dead animals. Vultures could usually be seen wheeling and turning in the air through the dust of the columns.

Signs of a large force having marched this way were evident: old camping grounds, distinguished by 'bully' beef and biscuit tins were passed, dead horses marked the lines of advance, and the smell from them was sickening. Their presence could be detected at a considerable distance, and one endeavoured by filling one's lungs as full as possible with air, and by holding one's nose to escape more than the first sniff. One's breath, however, generally gave out when one was exactly opposite the object, and it was then possible to know how a dead horse could smell.[31]

The scarcity of horses impeded British movements for the rest of the war. It was impossible to get enough in Africa, and the

82.

83 (*overleaf*). British column on the move.

army was forced to import animals from the USA, Australia, Austria and Hungary, but predominantly from the Argentine. In the end more than 211,000 animals were shipped in, as well as 100,000 mules, brought mainly from Spain, Italy and America. With their fodder came a weed from South America which still infests the land. Locals call it *khaki bos* (khaki bush), a reminder of the troops who swarmed over the country. The condition of the animals was poor; they were no match for the Boer ponies. The other factor which inhibited mobility was the huge quantity of supplies needed by columns. These were carried in slow, cumbersome wagon-trains, which frequently got into trouble.

Kitchener's next aim was to improve the tactics of column movement. He organized a series of country-wide sweeps called 'drives', which were planned with mathematical precision. Within a set area, a number of columns would begin moving in a carefully coordinated manner. Each would march in a designated direction until it reached the border of the adjacent territory. The troops would then retrace their steps to surprise any commandos moving into the empty space behind them. As soon as they had returned to their starting point they would turn about again and set off in a slightly different direction. It was an extraordinary concept of war. Thousands of men moved round and round the empty veld with clockwork precision as if in a complicated quadrille. At a pre-arranged moment a general surge, still circling, would be made towards the centre, rather like a whirlpool. (Since this was the

Southern Hemisphere, one likes to think they moved in an anti-clockwise direction!)

The first major drive began in March 1901. Kitchener divided the colony into four districts, each under the control of a general. Their instructions were to deal promptly with any enemy concentration, and 'to clear the country systematically of all horses, cattle, and supplies'. Kitchener had devised a complicated plan which was to be carried out along an imaginary line from Bultfontein and Winburg to Ficksburg. In the centre General Knox's columns began moving along the railway line. To the south General Lyttleton had three columns, two of which were commanded by officers who later became famous, Bruce Hamilton and Douglas Haig. In the east General Elliot had columns moving between Bethlehem and the Vaal. Meanwhile General Rundle was moving southwards to meet him. Throughout the regions fixed garrisons guarded the towns and railways, as well as a number of strategic points which had been carefully chosen to prevent Boers moving away from the driving columns. Elliot's movements were

84. Transport wagons frequently needed eight or nine 'spans' of oxen.

particularly energetic because there had been reports from the intelligence department that the Boers in the western Transvaal and the Free State were trying to make contact with each other. Advancing in a series of sweeping movements on a wide front towards a point just east of Heilbron, the columns then wheeled into a line moving north to drive the Boers towards drifts across the Vaal which had been strongly reinforced. The columns gradually abandoned their ox-wagons and travelled as lightly as they could, using packhorses and Cape carts.

The action is one of the most remarkable in the history of the British army. Beginning early in April, 11,000 men were pushed into a 10,000-square-mile territory and marched round and round until May, when winter was approaching. Most of the time the commandos kept their distance. Often they could clearly be seen a few miles off, trekking along with all their equipment. Only occasionally did the troops get close enough to attack.

Not all the drives were as big as this; smaller ones went on all the time. Life was hard on a drive, but there were occasional perks, as a young New Zealander, Frank Perham, reports:

85. A main column on the march.

April 7th (1901). We started out on trek at 10.30 a.m., travelled in a south-easterly direction till 8 p.m., camping for the night near a farmhouse. I was on night guard from 9.30 p.m. to 11.30 p.m., afterwards slept on Mother Earth in ordinary uniform and overcoat and did it freeze.

Next morning we moved off at 4 a.m.... We had great difficulty in getting the guns across on account of some of the team being unruly. One rider was thrown and almost drowned, and while the crossing was being negotiated the enemy was very active with their usual sniping tactics. My section was sent out to form a Cossack Post to deal with them.

After the crossing was completed we fed and watered our horses, then moved on and reached the Riet River at 1 p.m. We had trouble with donkey teams this time, teams owned by private firms who had taken advantage of our escort to get stores out to their establishments at Koffeefontein. The donkeys refused duty right in the centre of the ford and the greater part of the loads had to be removed from the wagons and carried across per 'manpower'.

The task of carrying the goods was assigned to an Infantry Corps, the Scottish Rifles, good whisky drinkers!

A fair part of the load comprised cases of whisky and somehow many of the cases had fallen to pieces. It was very tempting to the 'Scotties'

86. 'Peace and War': colonial troops visiting a farm. Notice the old man, women and children – the young men would have been on commando.

87. Colonial and Imperial troops waiting to attack.

and most of them became hopelessly drunk. They were brought before the heads and charged with being unfit for duty on the veldt, and were sentenced to seven days' CB. If the stuff they pinched had been Army property the charge would have been stealing, and the sentence about three months' hard![32]

From time to time most men managed to get into a town for a few days' leave, with all that went with it:

In addition, if at any time any of the boys wished to get over the traces they could be accommodated. Houses of ill-fame were numerous. However, these places were licensed by the authorities and subject to inspection, so were not considered to be places of ill-fame. A number of boys I know did pay visits to these places and some of them to their later regret.

I myself made a point of giving these places a wide berth and in consequence was at times subjected to quite a bit of slinging off, the parrot cry being 'Why be a Puritan? Come along with us and have a look anyway.' At last I said 'Right-oh, I'll come along.'

They took me to a place clean and well kept by all appearances. From the street we entered a cloak room and from there entered a large reception room with quite a number of chairs and couches. Also quite a number of girls, white, yellow and black. Leading from the reception room were a number of doors, presumably to small rooms designed for two. Anyway to finish a tale, I sat on a chair and immediately a buxom black lass perched herself on my knees, put her arms around my neck, and commenced whispering in my ears in broken English.

Doing a bit of quick thinking I said to myself, 'This is no place for you, Frank!' Sliding gently from under, I said, 'Excuse me, Girlie, while I go into the cloak room.' I walked sedately into the room, grabbed my coat and hat, stepped through the door into the street and made tracks back to camp. And that was that![33]

For the most part the experience of trekking throughout the war was one long grind:

On the march we used to move in columns of four, unless the veldt was broad and open, when we still kept our fours but moved the companies out to the right and left, so that we were really in a column of double companies moving in fours to a flank. This was a very good and

88. Searching for Boers. They were easy to see in the clear veld air, but were often out of range and could always keep ahead of the British columns.

simple formation, since the companies could open out or close in to the centre without difficulty, and at any time they were all handy and ready to move in any direction without the slightest delay. The battalion seldom or never moved in column of companies, as it was found that this was the most tiring formation of all in a long march, especially when the men were carrying a full kit. This full kit consisted of rifle with a magazine charged; haversack, with one day's complete rations and one day's issue of tea, sugar and biscuit, canteen and water bottle; sidearms and equipment with 10 rounds of ammunition; and a blanket strapped on the waistbelt at the back. All this totals up a good load but there was nothing that could have been dispensed with, the blanket, which was most cumbersome and unwieldy, being really as necessary as anything.

The officers were equipped the same as the men, and nearly all of them carried a rifle or carbine. This was a most necessary precaution, as there is no doubt the enemy invariably directed their fire on the officers, and of course anyone seen to be dressed differently to the men would be immediately spotted by the Boers . . .[34]

89. Troops entertaining themselves while waiting for a train.

On setting up camp, the first task was to find firewood and then to get something to eat. The men slept in their uniforms, wrapped in blankets. Many recorded spending a year or more in the veld without sleeping in a bed. Often the men had no change of clothes for weeks at a time:

90. Officers' sleeping arrangements on a drive.

Yesterday it was a curious sight to see us employing our leisured ease in stripping ourselves, scratching our bodies and carefully examining our shirts and underwear. A brutal lice(ntious) soldiery! Most of us have quite large families of these dependants upon us, a more euphonious term for them is 'Roberts' Scouts'. Men to whom the existence of such insects was once merely a vaguely-accepted fact and who would have brought libel actions against any persons insinuating that they possessed such things, after having been disillusioned of the idea that they were troubled with the 'prickly itch' were calmly, naked and unashamed, searching diligently for their tormentors in their clothes as to the manner born. Being fortunate enough to find an officers' servant with a bottle of Jeyes, I finally washed myself and clothes in a solution of it, so once again I am a free man, but the cry goes up 'how long' and echo repeats it. I have been told that the best way to get rid of these undesirable insects is to keep turning one's shirt inside out; by this means their hearts are eventually broken.[35]

91. Troops being moved by train.

The drives were not, however, really successful in reducing the Boers' ability to fight. The failure of the 'New Drives' was discussed and analysed endlessly at Kitchener's headquarters. Although most columns were moving faster than before, and the coordination between different columns was better, the country was too large for them to be able to trap small commandos. There were no geographical boundaries such as mountains or rivers against which they could be driven. On all sides the land was open. It was imperative that the country should be divided into smaller, better-defined areas in which columns would be more effective. It was suggested that the line of forts which had been erected to guard the railway be extended for this purpose, and Kitchener jumped at the idea.

The tactic of building a chain of forts came from the American war in Cuba. But this campaign, which had settled down to a series of inconclusive actions, had demonstrated effectively that forts by themselves could not prevent guerilla action. Kitchener's strategy was to integrate the function of fixed defensive units in fortified 'blockhouses' with that of mobile attacking units on the

92 (*top left*). Stone blockhouse on the railway line.

93 (*bottom left*). The first type of metal blockhouse.

94 (*right*). Positioning the prefabricated metal walls of a blockhouse after building a stone wall for the base.

drives. If the country could be divided into small areas by fortified lines, the Boers in each might be prevented from crossing to the next. It would then be possible to move columns by train into areas of Boer activity and attack them with precision and rapidity.

Roberts had set up lines of forts to guard the railway after the capture of Bloemfontein, when De Wet had begun systematically blowing up his lines of communication. In July 1900 work began on a series of trenches reinforced with stone walls or 'sangars' and barbed wire along the railway from the Cape. Detachments of men were encamped at intervals to defend each section. Near the rebuilt bridges a number of stone blockhouses were erected. They were two stories high and had a mount on the roof to which a machine-gun could be fitted. Entrance was by ladder through a door set about 7 or 8 feet above the ground. There were loopholes in the lower walls to allow the garrison to fire at ground level. The blockhouses took three months to erect and cost between £800 and £1,000 each.

In January 1901 the first metal blockhouse was put up. It was made of corrugated iron and built at Nelspruit by a contractor from Portuguese East Africa. Supports for the walls were made of two rows of wooden posts embedded in the ground about two feet apart to form a rectangle 10 by 15 feet. Inner and outer skins of corrugated iron were fitted to the posts, and the space between the two layers of metal filled in with stones and sand. Small loopholes were made by cutting openings in the walls and fitting metal plates between them. A corrugated-iron roof completed the building. Several prototypes of this kind of structure were built. The idea was to protect the garrison from rifle fire – the blockhouses were not strong enough to withstand an artillery bombardment.

Realizing that thousands of forts would be needed, Kitchener decided that prefabrication was the answer. The idea was passed on to the Royal Engineers to see if they could develop a design. Major S.R. Rice, who commanded the 23rd Field Company, took on the task and by February 1901 had come up with a plan for a circular blockhouse which could easily be prefabricated in sections and put together wherever needed along the railway line. He retained the idea of inner and outer skins of corrugated iron, to be separated by a layer of shingle sufficiently deep to stop rifle bullets. The outer skin was held in tension, the inner wall in compression, thus fixing the space between them. The two skins were linked together with 6 by 3 inch loopholes of tougher steel to produce a structure 13 feet 6 inches in diameter and 4 feet high which could withstand considerable stress. No wood was used in the walls because it was easily damaged by rifle fire. At first the blockhouses had square gabled roofs, also prefabricated, which were simply fixed on top of the walls when these had been bolted together. Later a circular roof was produced which gave rise to the name 'pepperpot blockhouse'. There was one small door made of thicker steel than the rest of the hut. Each fort slept six or seven men; stores and food were kept in the space under the roof. The forts cost £44 to begin with, but the price rapidly dropped to £16 when they were produced in large numbers.

Each blockhouse was surrounded by a stone wall about 2 feet high. Circular and radiating trenches were dug between forts, and stone sangars erected. This allowed the garrison to get outside and fight from a prepared defensive position if the Boers attacked. To complete the fortification, barbed-wire entanglements were placed between adjacent blockhouses. These were not simple fences but a mass of protective obstructions fashioned into a carefully worked out, complicated and seemingly impregnable defensive barrier. As building progressed the fences were strengthened by twisting together several strands of thick wire, and by using strong annealed wire which could not be severed with simple wire-cutters. The strands were held together by thick wire and metal stays which extended downwards into the ground, where they were anchored with heavy sandbags. Bells were attached to the fences to sound a warning if the fence was touched at night. There were even loaded rifles covering predetermined segments of the surrounding veld which fired automatically via trip-wires. Plans of the blockhouse lines show that they were arranged not as a simple line of forts, but in a complicated wave pattern with their windows angled away from each other so that rifle fire from one fort would be directed away from its neighbours. When a number of blockhouses opened up together with rifles and machine guns, the whole surrounding area would be swept systematically with bullets. Under such conditions it was almost impossible for Boers to slip between the forts.

As soon as Kitchener realized how easy they were to make he gave orders for a line of blockhouses to be erected between Kapmurden and Komatipoort, and this was done in January 1901. At first they were placed about one and a half miles from each other, but gradually the distance was shortened. The first blockhouse line was so successful that new ones were soon springing up along the railway lines all over the country. In June 1901 Kitchener had the idea of extending them across country between the railways. To build the new lines parties of Royal Engineers were sent out in convoys of ox-wagons carrying all the necessary prefabricated pieces. Between July and August 1901 the forts rapidly proved their worth, and Kitchener began to expand the system even more. Gradually a further 34 such cross-country lines were pushed across the veld. The longest ran for 175 miles along the railway line from Komatipoort to Wonderfontein and was garrisoned by 3,200 men. In the end Kitchener had nearly 50,000 men guarding more than 8,000 blockhouses. Lines were also laid around the big towns such as Pretoria, Johannesburg and Bloemfontein, which were thus made safe from Boer attack for the remainder of the war – there were no urban guerillas in the Boer War. By the end of 1901 the blockhouse lines were making it increasingly difficult for the Boers to attack the railways. They also served to separate the Boer leaders and prevent them uniting their commandos for coordinated action. Thus Botha's attacks were pretty much confined to the eastern Transvaal, De la Rey's to the western Transvaal and De Wet's to the Free State.

General Fuller, who fought in the First World War and later became famous for his advocacy of tanks, described the monotonous life led by a blockhouse garrison. Apart from sentry duty, there was nothing to do, and the men became jumpy and ill-tempered. Their only distractions were the convoys which passed from time to time. Towards the end automatic flares were invented which were designed to alert the whole line if Boers tried to get through. Even when nothing was visible in the dark, all the blockhouses that saw the signal would begin firing. Unfortunately the flares could be activated by animals wandering into the fence, and on one such occasion the firing spread up and down the line for about 100 miles.[36]

There is now only one metal blockhouse left standing in South Africa. It is in the garden of a modern private house on the edge of Bloemfontein and was probably the first blockhouse along the railway line. It is a pretty little top-heavy structure, and where there are scratches on it one can see that at one time it was painted an ochre red. The metal is much thicker (nearly half an inch thick) than the corrugated iron which has been used so extensively to build houses in South Africa, and its corrugations are much wider. It is dark inside because of the small windows, and one cannot imagine seven people living in it comfortably for any length of time. The building is soon to be removed to an outdoor museum in Bloemfontein, and at the same time the surrounding trenches, now covered with earth, will be dug up and examined.

There was a third element to Kitchener's strategy: having improved the drives and set up the blockhouse system, he now concentrated on a policy of 'land clearance', so that his columns could have an empty zone in which to get to grips with the enemy. This had other implications of equal importance: if the countryside were completely cleared, the commandos would find nowhere to replenish their stores and nowhere to rest.

95. Blockhouse protected by trenches reinforced with barbed wire.

96. A blockhouse garrison.

8. CONCENTRATION CAMPS

The destruction of farms began while Roberts was still in command. In March 1900 he offered to send home Boers who signed an oath of neutrality. Three months later he warned burghers that farms near sabotaged railway lines, or from which troops were fired upon, would be burned. In August a third proclamation informed fighting burghers that capture meant imprisonment and possible banishment from Africa for life, and that farms which had harboured them would be destroyed. Within weeks, groups of Boer refugees whose farms had been destroyed were seen moving about the veld. In early September *The Times* reported that a group of refugees had come into a British camp with cattle and wagonloads of belongings, looking for protection because they did not want to take part in further fighting. By November the number of refugees had increased dramatically and Roberts became worried that the problem might grow to unmanageable proportions. He issued instructions to the troops not to destroy farms unless specifically ordered to do so by a senior officer. Botha and the other Boer commanders let it be known that they welcomed the fact that the British were looking after the refugees, since this removed the responsibility from their hard-pressed commandos.

On the Boer side, Botha threatened action against burghers who left the commandos. When he met Kitchener he made the point clear: 'I am entitled to force every man to join me, and if they fail, to confiscate their property and leave their families on the veld.' When Kitchener took over, he was faced with a civilian population which continued to give as much help as it could to his opponents. With their assistance the Boer army could survive indefinitely in the countryside without help from the towns. Every district contained republican supporters. Even if they signed the oath of neutrality, they could not be trusted to remain neutral. A change of tactics was needed.

In December 1900 Kitchener issued a general memorandum which started the process of removing from the countryside anything which could be useful to the commandos. This policy was to lead eventually to the virtual destruction of the Boer farms and the death of a substantial part of the civilian population:

MEMORANDUM:

The General Commander-in-Chief is desirous that all possible means shall be taken to stop the present guerilla warfare. Of the various measures suggested for the accomplishment of this object, one which has been strongly recommended, and has lately been successfully tried on a small scale, is the removal of all men, women and children, and natives from the Districts which the enemy's bands persistently occupy. This course has been pointed out by surrendered burghers, who are anxious to finish the war, as the most effective method of limiting the endurance of the guerillas, as the men and women left on farms, if disloyal, willingly supply burghers, if loyal, dare not refuse to do so. Moreover, seeing the unprotected state of women now living in the Districts, this course is desirable to assure their not being insulted or molested by natives.

Lord Kitchener desires that General Officers will, according to the means at their disposal, follow this system in the Districts which they occupy or may traverse. The women and children brought in should be camped near the railway for supply purposes and should be divided in two categories, viz: 1st, Refugees, and the family of Neutrals, noncombatants and surrendered burghers. 2nd, Those whose husbands, fathers and sons are on commando. The preference in accommodation, etc., should, of course, be given to the first class. The Ordnance will supply the necessary tents and the District Commissioner will look after the food on the scale now in use.

It should be clearly explained to burghers in the field, that, if they voluntarily surrender, they will be allowed to live with their families in the camps until it is safe for them to return to their homes.

With regard to natives, it is not intended to clear Kaffir locations but only such Kaffirs and their stock as are on Boer farms. Every endeavour should be made to cause as little loss as possible to the natives removed and to give them protection when brought in. They will be available for any works undertaken, for which they will receive pay at native rates.

Pretoria, 21st December 1900[37]

Kitchener's 'land-clearance' policy gives an indication of the way his mind worked. He does not seem to have imagined its effect on the people who were to be thrown out of their homes. He saw only that it seemed the best way to deal with the commandos. It was imperative that the veld offer no possibility of refuge – therefore the countryside had to be laid waste. He was not trying to harm Boer families; he was not even trying to kill the burghers opposing him (there was never a 'body-count'). He was simply trying to weaken and slow down the commandos so that his drives could capture and disarm them. It is probable that he even considered the plan to be the most humane method of achieving this objective.

In every country area the local garrisons and columns set out to implement Kitchener's instructions. Small units began making their way from farm to farm burning or blowing up the houses.

97. Troops moving Boer women.

They removed all portable contents and took the Boer families to the nearest railway line. During the early months of 1901 the number of refugees increased rapidly. Once the process had begun, the situation developed inexorably into tragedy. Clearing the land effectively meant not only destroying the farms but removing anything living which could be of help to the enemy and killing all animals which could not be moved. The troops were often upset by what they were ordered to do:

The men belonging to the farm are always away and only the women left. Of these there are often three or four generations: grandmother, mother and family of girls. The boys over thirteen or fourteen are usually fighting with their papas. The people are disconcertingly like English, especially the girls and children – fair and big and healthy-looking. These folk we invite out onto the veldt or into the little garden in the front, where they huddle together in their cotton frocks and big sun-bonnets, while our men set fire to the house. Sometimes they entreat that it may be spared, and once or twice in an agony of rage they have invoked curses on our heads. But this is quite the exception. As a rule they make no sign, and simply look on and say nothing. One young women in a

98. Troops clearing furniture from a farmhouse.

farm yesterday, which I think she had not started life long in, went into a fit of hysterics when she saw the flames breaking out, and finally fainted away.

I wish I had my camera. Unfortunately it got damaged, and I have not been able to take any photographs. These farms would make a good subject. They are dry and burn well. The fire bursts out of windows and doors with a loud roaring, and black volumes of smoke roll overhead. Standing round are a dozen or two of men holding horses. The women, in a little group, cling together, comforting each other or holding their faces in each other's laps. In the background a number of Tommies are seen chasing poultry, flinging stones, and throwing themselves prostrate on maimed chickens and ducks, whose melancholy squawks fill the air. Further off still, herds and flocks and horses are being collected and driven off, while on top of the nearest high ground, a party of men, rifles in hand, guard against a surprise from the enemy, a few of whom can generally be seen in the distance watching the destruction of their homes.[38]

Some idea of what this experience was like for the victims can be gained from this description by Alie Badenhorst, whose hus-

band was a prisoner in Cape Town. It comes from her diary, which was translated by Emily Hobhouse:

> Monday morning came. They [the soldiers] were not yet gone; there stood the laager [camp]. About 11 o'clock Sister Hannie came to see me and Bettie with her. They said they should go to the English in order to ask them not to send us away. They went and told the English Officer that our husbands were prisoners of war and so they ought to let us stay where we were; the General replied to them that he was sorry, but that the order given to him was to bring in all the women and to drive them forth from their farms.
>
> Quickly they came back. It was a good half hour that they had to walk. They came straight to me and said: 'We all have to be taken away; from the English there is no hope, so best pack your things quickly.' At first I thought they must be joking me, but then I saw they were both crying; and looking out – all at once I could see wagons moving out from the camp ...
>
> I packed, and took bedding and tried to pack that also, but I was so crushed I did not quite know what I was doing, and they kept saying, 'Quick, quick', so I gathered a few necessaries together, and thus was I driven forth from my home. It was the 15th April 1901 never to be forgotten. My children cried; the two youngest boys were pale as death and held me fast; the little one kept crying for his chickens. I had to give him courage; and so we were carried, all of us, away.[39]

The refugees were taken to points of 'concentration', where camps could easily be built, protected, and supplied by rail. There were some men, too old for commando duty, amongst the refugees, but most were women and young children. The majority of the women had husbands who were still fighting. Some families were lucky enough to reach a town where they might have relatives to stay with. Town Boers with republican sympathies were not interned in the camps – there were no political prisoners in the modern sense.

It was not only whites who had their homes burned. By October 1901 Kitchener was reporting to the British government that 'native kraals' in areas where the Boers were fighting were having to be destroyed and the inhabitants moved to refugee camps. There is no doubt that blacks had been feeding and giving refuge to Boers. At first only black villages on the farms of Boers who were still fighting were 'cleared', but a number of officers who commanded columns recorded destroying black huts and villages wherever they might be useful to the enemy. By July 1901, when the systematic clearances were well under way, nearly 40,000 blacks, three quarters of them women and children, had been placed in camps. In the end there were more than fifty African camps. Some of these were attached to white camps, but the two groups of people were always carefully separated by camp administrators.

99. Burning a farm.

100. ' "October" and Garswood after looting a farm of a Boer who was at Senekal' (inscription on the back of this photograph from the album of an unnamed soldier).

101. Speeding up the destruction of farms.

Before

The explosion

After

Preparing the charge

102. British troops burning 'Kaffir Kraals' (1901).

As well as the refugees who had been forced to leave their homes, there were Boers who had simply decided not to continue fighting and were trying to escape Botha's reprisals. The resisting Boers called them 'hands-uppers'. Soon after Roberts captured Pretoria some burghers offered to act as scouts or intelligence agents for the British. It can be imagined how much they were disliked by their fellows. In the camps they were ostracized and stayed together for protection. From time to time a few would be let out of the camp and attached to a column as scouts. There were reports (mostly from Boer sources) that some had looted farms of burghers on commando. If caught by fighting Boers they were harshly dealt with: many were beaten up and some even shot.

A number of prominent Boers joined the British. Many, like De Wet's brother, thought that the war would ruin the whole country. Probably the first important Boer to suggest taking action against the war was the Free State general J. H. Olivier, who had defeated Gatacre's force at Stormberg junction but had eventually been cap-

103. Number 5 Wing of the Transvaal Scouts, commanded by A.P. Cronje (on the white horse in the front row). One of the rare photographs of Boers who fought for the British.

tured and shipped to Ceylon. Olivier offered to maintain the peace in his own district with a commando of men of his own choice, but this proposal was refused. A Burgher Peace Committee was formed in December 1900, and by February of the following year some of its members were offering to fight on the British side.

In September 1901 Kitchener decided to organize pro-British Boers into a force to fight the Boer army. Those from the Transvaal were known as 'National Scouts'; the Free Staters were called 'Orange River Volunteers'. Their two leading generals were Andries Cronje and Celliers. They were arranged into 'wings' of 50 to 150 men. Each wing was supervised by British officers to prevent defections to the commandos. The men signed up for periods of six months at a time. At first they were offered no payment, being allowed to take 'loot-money' instead, but this could be supplemented by 'presents' from headquarters for what was described as 'specially meritorious service'. Later they received the same rate as colonial volunteers: five shillings a day, rising to fifteen shillings for those who became officers. The volunteers were promised preferential treatment in the settlement of land when the war was over, and saw themselves as potential leaders of the post-war Boer nation, but there were never very many of them: by February 1902 less than 1,500 men had joined the British army from the Transvaal and only about 480 from the Orange Free State. They took part in a number of actions with British troops, mainly as scouts but sometimes as mounted infantry. However, the only action in which they were a real help to the army was on 2 February 1902, when a strong wing of National Scouts together with a British force captured Field Cornets Joubert, Du Toit and De Jager with 164 burghers.

The story of these Boer volunteers is a sad and in some cases disreputable one which has received little attention in Britain. Many of them were *bywoners*, or squatters, a class of poor farmers who had lost their own farms and lived on other men's property, paying for the privilege by helping with the farm work. Amongst Afrikaners they are remembered to this day with such hatred that it is almost impossible to get any information about them. During the war the intensity of feeling against them was so great that they had to be segregated within the camps. They were boycotted, often attacked, and, in spite of the religious nature of Boer society, even suffered church ostracism. In the end two camps were set aside for the families and men of the National Scouts. Scouts or Volunteers captured by the Boers were often summarily executed, and there is a report in the War Office papers by a British officer, Lieutenant H. Shipley, that twelve National Scouts had been castrated by their countrymen.

Meanwhile the destruction of farms continued. The reports from journalists who witnessed the burning and looting became more and more critical. Filson Young of the *Manchester Guardian* wrote as follows:

... the burning of houses that has gone on this afternoon has been a most unpleasant business. We have been marching through a part of the country where some mischievous person has been collecting and encouraging insurgents. And this afternoon in the course of about ten miles we have burned no fewer than six farmhouses. Care seems to have been taken that there was proper evidence against the owners, who were absent, and in no case were people actually burned out of their homes; but in one melancholy case the wife of an insurgent, who was lying sick in a friend's farm, watched from her sick husband's bedside the burning of her home 100 yards away. I cannot think punishment need take this wild form; it seems as though a kind of domestic murder were being committed while one watches the roof and furniture of a house blazing ... I stood till late last night before the red blaze and saw the flames lick around each piece of poor furniture – the chairs and tables, the baby's cradle, the chest of drawers containing a world of treasure; and when I saw the poor housewife's face pressed against the window of the neighbouring house, my own heart burned with a sense of outrage.

104. Boer women being taken to a concentration camp.

The effect on those of the colonial troops who, in carrying out these orders to destroy, are gratifying their feeling of hatred and revenge, is very bad. Their discipline is far below that of the Imperial troops, and they soon get out of hand. They swarm into the houses, looting and destroying, and filling the air with high sounding cries of vengeance, and yesterday some of them were complaining bitterly that a suspected house, against the owner of which there was not sufficient evidence, was not

105. A concentration camp. Early
camps had wooden huts like those in
the centre; when these ran out large
tents were used. Later only circular
bell-tents were available.

delivered into their hands. Further, if these farms are to be confiscated (as the most vindictive loyalists desire), and then given over to settlers, why burn the houses? The new occupant will only have to build another homestead, and building is a serious matter where wood and the means for dressing stone are so very scarce as here. The ends achieved are so small – simply an exhibition of power and punishment which (if it be really necessary) could be otherwise inflicted, and the evils as one sees them on the spot, are many.[40]

The women and children were loaded on to wagons and the long trek to the camps began. Within a few months more than 30,000 had been forcibly moved from their farms in the western Transvaal in small groups of 50 or 100 at a time. They suffered a great deal on the way.

... about mid-day they come in sight of what makes the stoutest heart quail with fear – the concentration camp ... at Volksrust. No one on that convoy had lived too far out of the way to hear some report of the miseries of such a place.

Nearer they come and are able to distinguish the rows and rows and rows of tents. Just as they are close to the gate a bare wagon drawn by horses meets them, on it are six coffins, two large and four small ...

Brought into the camp they are first directed to the Commandant's tent. The names, ages, addresses etc.... are booked. All of them having to stand during the weary time of waiting, till the last name is put down and each family gets a ration ticket.

They are then escorted to their homes ... They have to walk a couple of hundred yards down the broad street between the rows of tents, following the wagon carrying their luggage. At last they stand before a bell tent; their goods are thrown down and there they are left to look after themselves.[41]

Concentration camps in the Boer War must not be confused with the German camps of the Second World War. The British camps were set up for an entirely different reason and were meant to house the refugees in comfort and safety. However, their administration soon ran into such difficulties that conditions became very bad. The health of the occupants was a major problem. The biggest worry was that an epidemic of typhoid would break out, as it had during Roberts's advance. When illness did begin to sweep through the camps, specific anti-typhoid measures were instituted.

Conditions in the early camps varied greatly, and Kitchener set about remedying deficiencies. The living quarters and food were carefully supervised. Each camp was run by a Superintendent, with a store-keeper, a few clerks, a medical officer, a dispenser, a matron and a few nurses. Extra medical assistance was provided by camp inmates, who were paid for their help. The whole system cost the British taxpayer a considerable amount of money, but by careful administration this was kept to a minimum. Between January and November 1902 expenditure on the camps was about £400,000, with the daily cost at about six shillings a head.

The administration was instructed to find employment for as many of the refugees as possible. They were paid for various camp jobs, some families receiving up to £20 a month. Eventually, even when no work needed to be done, three hours' compulsory labour a day was imposed on adult males – for their own good, according to the Victorian notion. There was little for the men and children to do, but the women worked hard looking after the others and trying to keep their possessions in good order. As conditions worsened, more of their time was spent nursing the sick.

Camp shops sold food, clothing and a few luxuries to those who could afford them, at prices regulated by martial law. When winter came additional clothing, contributed by various charitable organizations, was handed out. Some lucky refugees who had surrendered voluntarily had been able to bring their cattle and livestock with them. They were allowed to keep the animals on nearby grazing land and to guard them so that they were not

106. Women arriving in a camp.

stolen at night by commandos. However, the majority of families had few possessions except a few pieces of furniture and the clothes they had been wearing when they were taken from home. Schools were set up in tents, or in more solid wooden huts when these were available. Books were provided and teachers recruited. Even some of the Boer women took advantage of these facilities.

Thus conditions in many camps were initially not too bad. However, things soon began to go wrong. At first the problem was a shortage of supplies. By 7 December 1900, Milner, the Governor-General of Cape Colony, who had by then taken over responsibility for the camps, was writing:

We were suddenly confronted with a problem not of our making, which it was beyond our power properly to grapple, and no doubt its vastness was not realized soon enough. The first of the suffering resulted from inadequate accommodation. It was originally meant to house the refugees in wooden shelters, but there was not sufficient material for enough of them to be made.[42]

107. Boer family installed in their tent. Many such photographs were taken, probably to reassure husbands that their families were well.

Milner, of course, represented the civil administration in South Africa. The Boer War was probably the first situation in which the British army set up a formal military administration to see to civilian affairs. Soon after the annexation of the Orange Free State by Roberts in 1900, a military governor had been appointed. He and his legal and financial aides assumed responsibility for the residents of the conquered territory, who became British citizens when the proclamation of annexation was issued. In August of

108 (*top*). Tanks of boiled water in a camp.

109 (*bottom*). Washing facilities in Norval's Pont Camp.

the same year the Transvaal Republic was annexed. The Boers claimed that the annexations were invalid, since their forces had not been defeated. It is still a controversial point. Nevertheless, throughout the war the British authorities had accepted that it was their duty to look after the civilian population. During the next twelve months Milner, as Governor-General of the largest British colony in South Africa, began taking an increasing interest in the administration of the annexed territories. In February 1901 he left Cape Town for Johannesburg, where he began setting up a comprehensive civilian administration. In the same month Kitchener asked him to take over control of the camps from the military: looking after large numbers of women and children was difficult, and Kitchener felt that he could not spare officers and men for the task. However, it was not until November 1901 that all the camps came under Milner's direct control.

Milner inherited the accommodation problem from the army. At first refugees had been housed in prefabricated wooden huts, but the supply was soon exhausted. Square canvas marquees were found to be nearly as good, but they were expensive and difficult to obtain. In the end the camps were made up for the most part of rows of bell-tents. One was assigned to each family. Alie Badenhorst describes the scene in her camp:

... one had to make little fireplaces in front of the tents – tents that must serve as sitting-room, pantry, bedroom and dining-room in one, and they were of a size that were there but one small bed and a table therein, there was no room to turn; and when there was a number of children as well! Most of the poor women had not even brought a bedstead with them because they were seized in such haste. When we came the women received eatables three times a week. Tuesday, meat; Wednesday, meal, sugar, coffee, salt; and Saturday again meat. The food stores were not near the camp, quite ten minutes' walk, and they had to carry it all. For each person there was 7 lbs of meal a week, no green food, and no variety; the sugar was that black stuff which we always give to our horses for worms; the coffee was some mixture, no one could rightly say what coffee it was, some said acorns, others dried peas – but it was all a very sore trial for us to bear, we, who were so used to good food – vegetables, milk and mealies. It came bitterly hard to us.[43]

There was a strict rationing system for food. Expert medical authorities had been consulted to make sure the quantity and quality of the inmates' diet was sufficient for them to remain healthy.

Early in 1901 critical accounts of conditions in the camps began to reach Britain. Opposition papers were full of worrying reports about the way they were being run. Inspectors were ordered to visit the camps and report to the government. However, after the publication of Emily Hobhouse's heart-rending book and articles, it was felt that something more was needed to counteract the

110. The winter of 1901.

allegations of mismanagement. A commission of women was sent out to visit all the camps, and the government produced a Blue Paper with detailed reports of the situation in each. By this time there were 45 concentration camps. They varied in size, but the largest contained more than 5,000 people.

There now occurred an unexpected complication: the winter of 1901 was severe:

During the winter of 1901 a blizzard passed over the High Veldt, the site of so many concentration camps, in the Balmoral District, and overtook a young Lieutenant, W. St Clare McLaren of the First Argyle and Sutherland Highlanders ... with his men.

They were without shelter, the commissariat wagons being some way ahead, and crept under a tarpaulin for protection from the fierce and bitterly cold blast.

During that awful night, Mr McLaren took off his overcoat to cover up the perishing body of his Major, and when morning came he was found dead with five of his men, while around them, stiffly frozen, lay the bodies of 600 mules.[44]

Only the old and the ill died of the cold in the camps, but sickness began to spread like a dark stain amongst the children, and soon reached the adults too. With frightening rapidity the

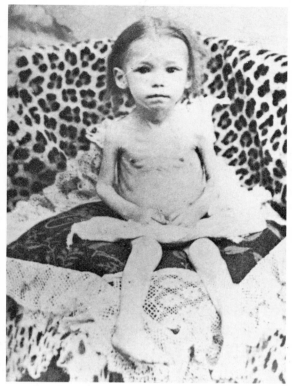

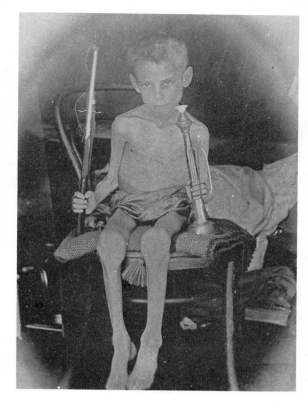

111*a*, *b* and *c*.

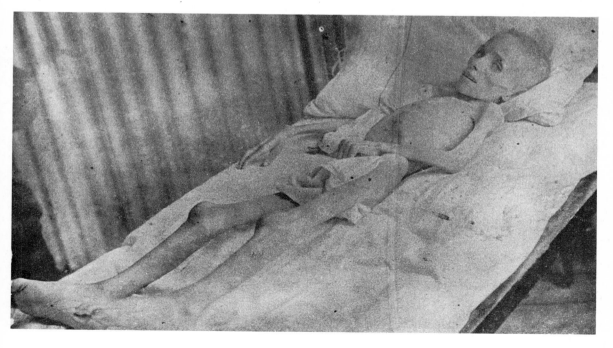

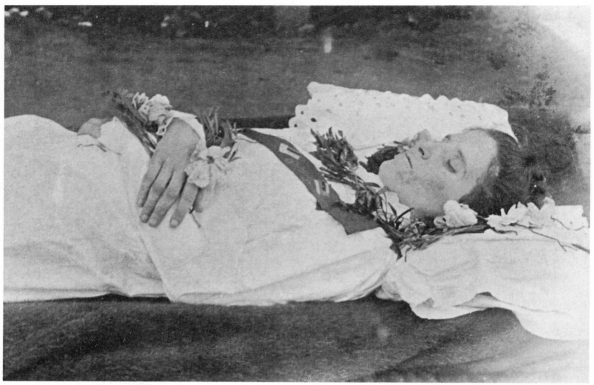

112a.

numbers of sick began to climb in all the camps. Deaths began to be reported in increasing numbers. The camp at Brandfort had the highest death rate during the worst month. By October 1901, of the 113,506 registered refugees in the camps, 3,156 had died, most of them children. Spring came, and then summer, but the deaths continued. By January the following year there were still 1,800 deaths a month.

Alie Badenhorst wrote:

There was at this time no chance for us to hear anything from outside: we could see no telegrams and heard only that which we could not listen to with certainty; we only learned bits here and there from women brought in by the columns, or from a convoy which brought in food. It was most miserable for me when the columns came in, for they always drove so many cattle before them and these, gathered in their hundreds and needing food and water, bellowed until the sound was heart-rending. I thought sometimes that I must fly to some place where I could not hear the sound of their misery, the neighing of the foals, the bleating of the sheep – it seemed in truth as if God's hand were too heavy upon us, both man and beast. O God, dost Thou strive with us in Thine anger and chastise us in Thy wrath. Be merciful and wipe us not from the face of the earth.[45]

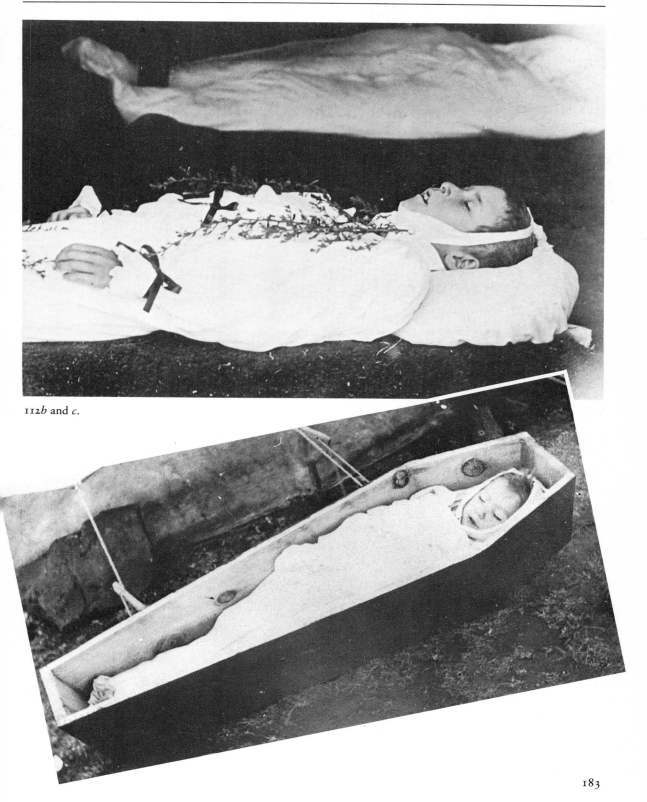

112*b* and *c.*

An entry in her diary during December 1901 reads:

> In our country ... December was a month of pleasure, but now it
> opened instead with sorrow. For it was this day, the 1st December, that
> old Tant' Hannie died ... It was hard to believe she had gone from
> amongst us, for whom she had filled so large a place ... I never thought
> with my eyes to see so much misery ... tents emptied by death. I went
> one day to the hospital and there lay a child of nine years to wrestle
> alone with death. I asked ... where I could find the child's mother. The
> answer was that the mother died a week before, the father is in Ceylon,
> that very morning her sister of 11 died. I pitied the poor little sufferer as
> I looked upon her ... There was not even a tear in my own eyes, for
> weep I could no more. I stood beside her and watched until a stupefying
> grief overwhelmed my soul ... I lamented like the prophet, 'I am the man
> that has seen affliction by the rod of His wrath.'[46]

The chaplain of the Bethulie concentration camp kept a diary
between August 1901 when he joined the staff of the camp and
the end of October when he collapsed physically and mentally. It
makes harrowing reading – the days filled with suffering and
death, the nights broken by shrill whistles calling for another
corpse to be taken to the mortuary tent:

> Very trying afternoon among the dying. One woman just gave her last
> when I entered to pray for her; lamentation. Roaring lion, because of the
> crowd of inquisitives; stood at the doorway and addressed them; said I
> was ashamed of their conduct; boiled over. Simply will not stand such
> things ...
> A funeral to me is the most fatiguing duty; more so when one has to
> give an address at the graves; and there is no time for preparation except
> on the march to the burying ground. I am getting restless, for I am forced
> absolutely to rely on impromptu grace. I tremble when I think what I risk
> each day.
> O for a change of work! The continual cry is 'Minheer, kom tog heer'
> [Sir, please come here], 'Minheer, gaat tog daar' [Sir, please go there],
> and one grows weary of scenes of suffering and sorrow ... always face to
> face with helpless, hopeless, impotent despairing; always face to face with
> Decay, Change, Death; always the same close, stifling, little tent.[47]

What was causing the deaths? At first doctors feared that typhoid had started up again and got into the camps. Strict orders
were issued by camp commandants not to allow in food or water
which might be contaminated. Fresh vegetables were forbidden.
Water was boiled and kept in large sealed tanks. Fresh meat from
outside was stopped; tinned beef from America was issued. A
careful watch was kept on the tins of meat, samples of which
were constantly tested to ensure that they were free of infection.

However, in spite of all the precautions the death toll continued
to rise. Rumours began circulating in the commandos that Boer

women and children were being systematically poisoned with infected meat. People in the camps reported that ground glass could be seen in the sugar supplied by the authorities. This was probably the blue aniline dye crystals which were then usually added to white sugar to make it more attractive. Questions about the deaths began to be asked by newspapers in England. Pro-war journalists wrote that the main cause of the illness was the lack of cleanliness of the Boer families, who were said to be quite unused to bathing. They added that when children became ill the mothers refused modern medical treatment. It is certainly true that Boer mothers often fought desperately to prevent their children being taken into the hospitals, where the death rate was very high, and preferred trying the old Boer remedies. They were probably right. Putting all the children together may have spread infection, and there was certainly no specific treatment for the diseases which were sweeping through the camps.

Another point made by doctors in England was that the condition of the country had been made so dangerous by the war that epidemics were inevitable. The administration suggested that the death rate would have been much higher in the civilian population if the women and children had been left to fend for themselves. As we shall see, this is a view which cannot be accepted. In any case the British authorities had assumed responsibility for the Boer families who had been forcibly moved from their homes. It was disingenuous of them to disclaim the consequences of their own actions.

The camp doctors and administrators appear not to have recognized the main cause of illness, although this was obvious to Boer mothers like Alie Badenhorst:

Worst of all – because of the poor food, and having only one kind of food without vegetables – and then that tinned beef – there came a sort of scurvy amongst the people. They got a sore mouth and a dreadful smell with it; in some cases the palate fell out and the teeth, and some of the children were full of holes or sores in the mouth. And then they died... The mothers might never buy them anything; there were usually vegetables to be bought, but they might not go out of the camp, the head of the camp was strict...

Today ... I am feeling somewhat better, but in the camp dying still goes on. Scarletina is raging there and daily several are being buried. In our country scarletina is not a dangerous sickness, often the children do not go to bed ... they just lie down; but these poor children are so weak, not having had proper food for so long. The meat was miserable stuff ... tinned beef once a week and once mutton.[48]

The Boers in the camps were certainly given enough to eat. The problem was that their diet was deficient in essential vitamins. This was an age which knew little about community resistance to disease, still less about nutrition and virtually nothing about vitamins. In 1900 doctors knew that abnormal diets could cause diseases: scurvy and rickets had been recognized for hundreds of years and beri-beri had been described by Dutch doctors as far back as the middle of the seventeenth century. Captain Cook had used citrus fruit to prevent scurvy on board ship in the 1770s, and twenty years before the Boer War Japanese doctors had overcome an outbreak of beri-beri in the navy by adding fresh meat and vegetables to the sailors' diet. But the idea of 'malnutrition' rather than 'undernutrition' was in its infancy. It was not until the pioneer experiments of medical research workers nearly a decade after the British concentration-camp deaths that the importance of trace substances in the diet became clear.

There was another unrecognized factor predisposing the children to infection. The Boer families interned in the camps had lived on farms or in small widely separated villages. They met only occasionally, and then for short periods. Sick children would be left at home. Thus not only did the farm families live a healthy life and eat well, but children were not normally exposed to infectious diseases in the way that those of Victorian city-dwellers were. It was therefore precisely those with least resistance to disease who were now moved into crowded, unsanitary conditions with inadequate shelter and a diet which could only result in severe malnutrition. When their physical state had been lowered sufficiently, the simple illnesses of childhood became lethal. Then when epidemics of scarlet fever, gastroenteritis and measles began, the doctors compounded their error, systematically starving the camp inmates of the vitamins which were so badly needed and doing everything in their power to keep everyone together in the camps so that disease would not spread to the towns. The immunity of women was also drastically reduced, and tuberculosis spread like whooping cough.

The exact number of Boers who died in the camps is still the subject of argument. After the war the official archivist of the Transvaal government, P. L. A. Goldman, fixed the figure at 27,927, of which more than 26,000 were women and children. Even the British records agree on slightly more than 20,000 deaths. Since the entire Afrikander population in the two Republics was a good deal less than 100,000, the loss was catastrophic. Nearly a quarter of the women and children of the old Republics were dead. Nor were these the only camp deaths. A mortality rate which passed almost unnoticed in Britain and South Africa was that of black women and children. In her book *The Brunt of War*, Emily Hobhouse records that 13,315 Africans died in concentration camps. This is probably an underestimate. The most modern medical advice for the care of camp inmates had been sought, and for the most part camp administrators had done their best. Yet, when all was said and done, an act had been perpetrated in the

113. Black 'refugees' being taken to a camp.

114. Black 'refugees' entering a camp.

name of the British people which is still viewed by Afrikaners as a crime. They cannot forget it.

Even in strategic terms the camps were a failure. Although conditions in the desolate veld made life hard for the fighting men, those who remained continued to fight. In a perverse way the losses in the camps became the very reason for them to go on. The harshness of their lives, their diminishing numbers and the extent of their families' sufferings only strengthened their determination to continue the war.

Through all this sordid mess there was one Briton who stood out on the side of humanity and reason. Emily Hobhouse was the fifth child of Reginald Hobhouse, Rector of St Ives, and was 39 years old when the war started. Much influenced by her uncle, Lord Hobhouse, who held strong views against the war, she joined the South African Conciliation Committee when it was formed. The farm burnings and the development of the refugee camps which were reported in the newspapers towards the end of 1900 became the focus of the Committee's interest. In November a Cape Town Relief Committee applied to have women and children in the camps released if they had friends in town who would look after them, or if their expenses could be paid by subscription, but the military authorities refused to let them go. Emily Hobhouse decided to go out to Africa to see what she could do. She wrote to Lord Lansdowne and Mr Chamberlain and received replies expressing their sympathy with the objectives of a new charity to be called the South African Women and Children Distress Fund. Both politicians promised to write asking Sir Alfred Milner to give her every assistance. She arrived in Cape Town on 27 December 1900, and Milner invited her to lunch. When she insisted on a formal interview he granted her fifteen minutes, but ended up extending this to more than an hour. He agreed to her visiting the camps south of Bloemfontein with a Boer woman, but would not allow them to go further north. They travelled from camp to camp making careful notes of the conditions in each. Early in May she returned home and published her findings in newspaper articles and in a pamphlet issued by the South African Conciliation Committee.

The uproar that followed Emily Hobhouse's revelations further polarized opinion in Britain. She was almost overcome by the bitter outcry of her critics, many of whom said that her facts were inaccurate. However, she did not stop her campaign, and in October 1901 returned to the Cape. While she was at sea martial law was proclaimed in the Cape Colony and when she arrived she was immediately arrested and deported on Kitchener's personal order. He had her taken off the ship as soon as it docked and escorted by nurses straight to a returning ship. She protested violently, and the authorities were forced to send stretcher-bearers to carry her. She wrote immediately to Milner, Kitchener and the Military Commander of Cape Town, but was kept imprisoned on board the ship until it sailed. On her return to England the newspapers gave wide coverage to what had happened. The *Manchester Guardian* in particular published a strong condemnation of her treatment.

Emily Hobhouse was not able to return to South Africa for the rest of the war, but her efforts had a major effect on public opinion in Britain and forced the government into action. The deputation of women they sent out to investigate the situation in the camps corroborated her findings, which compelled the authorities to improve conditions. After the war she went back to South Africa and helped in the Boer resettlement. Emily Hobhouse's work puts her amongst the first rank of Britons of her age, and to the Boers she was more than just a social worker. She is buried with De Wet and Steyn in Bloemfontein, at the memorial to the women who died in the camps. No greater honour can be given by the Afrikaans nation.

9. THE BITTER END

In the second half of 1901, as winter came to an end and the weather improved, the deaths in the camps began to diminish. With the spring, thoughts in both armies turned to the coming summer campaign. In the British headquarters there was no reason to believe that the Boers would be any less determined to resist than they had been the previous year, and quite suddenly Kitchener's patience began to fail. His policy of 'drives and destruction' had not succeeded. The hard core of Boer fighters were as active as ever and their leaders seemed to lead charmed lives. Something more had to be done to end the fighting – whether a real attempt at conciliation or even harsher suppression. Kitchener chose the latter course, suggesting a number of stringent measures which could be taken. He urged permanent exile for burghers and their families who did not surrender immediately. They could be resettled in the East Indies or Madagascar, where they would probably be accepted by the Dutch and French authorities. He also raised the possibility of breaking the Boer spirit by surreptitiously fostering the split between pro- and anti-war factions until a situation bordering on civil war was created – though he added that he was not certain that sufficient animosity could be artificially maintained. The Cabinet came out sharply against such underhand methods. In September, however, he received authorization to announce that the government demanded nothing less than unconditional surrender from both republican forces, and that all burghers who remained with their commands after the 15th would be banished for life from South Africa. As expected, the Boers simply ignored the proclamation. By November Kitchener was writing leters to Roberts complaining about the ineffectiveness of political measures to stop the fighting. His vexation must have been persuasive, because Roberts actually offered to take back the command so that Kitchener could go to India. Kitchener replied that he wanted to see it through, however long it lasted.

Kitchener may have felt frustrated, but his tightening grip on the country *was* having an effect. His headquarters had become the centre of a vast machine over which he kept strict personal control. 'He was preeminently a great organizer,' wrote Erskine Childers in *The Times History of the War in South Africa*. 'To view the guerilla war mainly as a problem of organization was in his blood.'[49] Kitchener was renowned for obsessional thorough-

115. Spring in the veld: the gardens.

ness and made ceaseless efforts to catch the remaining Boer commandos in the annexed territories. But still their attacks continued. However, in the large towns, ringed by heavily garrisoned blockhouses, life returned to normal. In December the Johannesburg Stock Exchange reopened. Business began to recover as the Uitlanders returned and the shops began trading, but the countryside was a scene of desolation. Flowers grew in the ruined farmhouses; nowhere was shelter to be found.

The last few months of the year saw continuous sporadic fighting in the annexed territories, but it was in the Cape that the most notable events took place. Jan Smuts had been born in the Cape. From the beginning he had expressed the opinion that the Boers' best chance of winning lay in an invasion aimed at inciting rebellion amongst Afrikanders in the British territory. In spite of the earlier failures of Botha, De Wet, Hertzog, Kritzinger and the

116. Spring in the veld: the farms.

smaller commandos, by the middle of 1901 Smuts had convinced De la Rey that it was not too late to try once more, and that he, Smuts, stood the greatest chance of success. Smuts possessed three advantages which the others lacked: he was closely associated with Cape Afrikander leaders; he had held high administrative office in the Transvaal; and his oratory and writing could be very persuasive. But the mision was hazardous. All along his proposed route to the Cape, Kitchener's columns were constantly on the move. Smuts therefore planned that his commando should traverse the Free State in small groups and reassemble in the Cape, where he could recruit volunteers. His aim was nothing less than the capture of Cape Town itself. It was hoped that the combination of military success in the colony and pressure of world opinion would open a chance of peace without loss of independence.

On 16 July Smuts's commando set off in four groups. Even the march through the Transvaal was difficult. Kitchener's columns were constantly sweeping the area: Steyn himself had only escaped by luck during the first week of July, when most of his headquarters staff had been captured. Soon after Smuts set out, Kitchener learned of his move from the intelligence department and dispatched a column to intercept him. Crossing the Transvaal had been bad enough, but once Smuts reached the Vaal river it seemed almost impossible to evade the British. He was nearly captured while fording the river, when he went back to help others across; he came even closer to capture two days later when his camp was attacked at night by 200 South Australians. In the uproar he got away by running as fast as he could without boots. It took him days to recover from the injuries to his feet.

In fact, Smuts had wandered by chance into one of the largest and best organized drives yet orchestrated by Kitchener. In the depopulated wilderness 15,000 men in 17 columns were moving in complicated spirals, constantly changing direction. In addition a number of smaller groups were being used as 'stop columns' to block the spaces between the main columns and catch Boers trying to infiltrate. In small groups, suffering intensely at night from the cold, Smuts's commando slogged on for nearly a month through the wheeling maze of columns. It is difficult to imagine how they managed to get through, but it must not be thought that the 300-mile ride was solely one of evasion, for on numerous occasions the commando fought off attacks. Smuts was continually losing men, but nevertheless on 3 September 1901 he slipped across a drift at Klarwater and entered the Cape.

Smuts had planned to proclaim a new Boer Republic in the western Cape with assistance fom the locals and reinforcements from the Transvaal and the Free State. As a start he proclaimed himself 'Commander-in-Chief'. However, the Free Staters could give him little support; Kritzinger was unable to link up with him

117. General Jannie Smuts on commando.

and was forced by the drives to break his commando into small units; the rebels had no horses and could not join him. The invasion had failed in its main objective, but when the summer started and Christmas came Smuts was virtually in control of a large though empty area of the north-western Cape.

He set about reorganizing the commandos in the region as De la Rey had done in the western Transvaal. The area was divided between four Vecht-Generals: Malan to the east, Van de Venter to the south, Lategan to the north, and Maritz near the border with German South-West Africa. The latter was the most important sector. Through it a Boer commando established effective communication with the outside world for the first time since Komatipoort had fallen. The commandos themselves were restructured. The fighting unit was now a squad of twelve under a

corporal. Groups of squads controlled by field-cornets made up the commandos, which retained the commandant as senior officer. Smuts imposed strict military discipline: alcohol was forbidden except by special permission from an officer; the civilian population and prisoners were not to be ill-treated; looting was forbidden; burghers who were absent without leave would be punished. He drew up a formal system of penalties: field-cornets were empowered to impose a punishment known as 'pack-saddles'; councils of commandants and field-cornets could order a convicted burgher to be lashed; spies could only be executed after conviction by a specially constituted military court. The new attitude was reflected in their costume, which became more like a military uniform with its dark jacket, riding breeches and crossed bandoliers or belts across the chest.

In January 1902 Smuts issued a proclamation to civilians in the

118. *a* Waiting for a dawn attack in the guerilla war; *b* An attack: mounted infantry advance; *c* The advance.

b

a   c

region he had occupied warning them not to obey British laws. He wrote to De la Rey saying that although the rebellion was going more slowly than had been anticipated, he was still confident of victory if the Transvaal would send him reinforcements. About this time some of his political pamphlets were published in Europe and sent to prominent pro-Boers in England. The letter to De la Rey was accompanied by a 12,000-word dissertation on the Boer attitude to the war. How did he ever find the time? He was certainly not shirking his military duties. On the 26th he wrote again to De la Rey, telling him of a plan to march south and east, deep into the populated areas of the Cape, to make contact with his family and the Afrikander leaders, but there was no real chance of this. In the Republics the 'bitter end' had almost arrrived. Botha's and De Wet's commandos were near the end of their tether and British troops were still arriving in South Africa. As Smuts

a

c

b

119. *a* 'Bitter-enders'; *b* A 'bitter-
ender' catching a few moments' sleep
in the middle of the day when it was
safest; *c* Sniper sniped.

realized this his mood darkened. Unlike the other Boer leaders he held himself aloof from his men, and now he seemed to withdraw even further. But he was not a man to give in easily.

Since he could not move south, Smuts headed north towards the copper mines at O'kiep and its surrounding villages. First he attacked and captured the villages, having blown up their defending forts with home-made dynamite grenades – the first time these were used in the war. Then he turned on O'kiep, but its commander refused to surrender. It was the beginning of April when Smuts began besieging the town. By day a constant rifle fire was aimed high at the town; at night the burghers atttacked the forts. But they could not penetrate the defences: Major Dean, the manager of the Cape Copper Company in the town, had prepared them well. At intervals along the five-mile perimeter were fifteen strong blockhouses connected by wire with high stone sangars. The garrison, commanded by an Australian, consisted of nearly 1,000 men with a nine-pounder gun and a Maxim. They managed to get a message through to General French, who immediately sent columns by sea to Port Nolloth, less than sixty miles away, which was connected to the town by rail. For nearly a week Smuts kept up his attacks without being able to break through. At one point he even tried unsuccessfully to roll a railway wagon stuffed full of dynamite into the town. Two blockhouses were captured, one by Maritz, an immensely strong ex-policeman who stood on the shoulders of another man and hurled a twenty-pound dynamite grenade through the roof. The town itself was never captured – Smuts received a letter from Kitchener requesting him to come to Vereeniging to discuss a peace settlement. He was taken to Port Nolloth and boarded a battleship for Simonstown, to the considerable interest of the British soldiers and sailors on board.

During January and February 1902 Kitchener's relentless pressure gradually wore down the Boer forces. On all sides there was a clamour for peace. The columns were moving ceaselessly in every region, and continued to do so even when negotiations began. In February De Wet just managed to escape from one of the new drives. At about this time an incident occurred in the Vryheid district which caused great indignation among the Boers. A party of Zulus crept up on a farmhouse where 59 Boers were sleeping and murdered the whole party. The Boers complained bitterly and pointed out that the British were using armed blacks in the blockhouses and for the drives. This was true. But the Boers also received help from blacks during the first battles and photographs of Beyer's commando show armed blacks.

Meanwhile changes were taking place in the Cape. Cecil Rhodes died, and Milner tried to have Kitchener, who seemed to be losing his animosity for the enemy, removed. Milner was particularly worried by the Boers' ability to continue fighting. The whole

120. Stephanus Houptfleisch, a 'bitter-ender', in Pretoria immediately after the war.

a

situation might have remained in limbo for months if the Dutch Prime Minister had not made an unexpected offer to mediate. Letters discussing a possible settlement were exchanged between the Dutch and British governments, and on 20 March a copy of the correspondence was handed to Botha by a British officer while he was attending a church service. He agreed to a meeting of Boer leaders, and commandants were sent letters giving them free passage to Klerksdorp. Kitchener had great hopes of bringing the negotiations to a successful conclusion. He had been under great strain for many months and had nearly collapsed two weeks earlier on hearing that Lord Methuen had been wounded and captured by De la Rey in the eastern Transvaal. Methuen, one of the most senior British officers in South Africa, had been reduced to leading a column in De la Rey's district. The reason for this is not clear, since he had not done worse than other commanders during Kitchener's time. The incident occurred while he was trying, with inexperienced troops, to recapture guns which De la Rey had taken from a convoy a few days earlier. Soon after daybreak they were surrounded by De la Rey's commando. The Boers formed up in five mounted lines and galloped straight at the British position, firing rifles from the hip. Methuen held out for a

121. *a* Armed blacks in a British column; *b* Armed blacks with General Beyer's commando.

b

couple of hours, though most of his mounted men fled when they saw the Boers approaching. He was wounded in the thigh, which was fractured. De la Rey came to see him and treated him with great kindness, even sending a message to his wife, and a short time later the Boers sent him back to the British lines. His injury was, however, a severe one: he used a stick for the rest of his life.

This was not the last Boer attack. On the morning of 11 April, while Kitchener was looking for De la Rey, who was away from his commando, one of the latter's assistants, General Kemp, attacked a column sixty miles from Klerksdorp. Kemp tried to use De la Rey's tactic of charging on horseback, but the troops unexpectedly stood their ground and he was forced to break off the attack, leaving nearly 50 Boers dead and more wounded. An old commandant, Potgieter, died within feet of the British guns, and the Boers later blamed Kemp for this untimely death. Potgieter was not, however, the last man to die. This honour is awarded by Conan Doyle, who was an army medical officer and wrote a book about the war, to a young lieutenant of the Seaforths named Sunderland, who had only recently left Eton. He was ambushed near Frederikstad, and when his horse had been shot from under him, his mounted Boer attackers played with him, chasing him for

nearly a mile and finally riding in circles round him before shooting him.

On 9 April the Boer leaders assembled at Klerksdorp to discusss a possible end to the fighting. After some discussion they agreed to meet Kitchener in Pretoria, where they presented him with a six-point plan. Most of the clauses were not controversial, but Steyn, who had come in spite of illness, was anxious to get Kitchener to acknowledge independence for the Boer states. Kitchener could not agree to this and advised the Boers to submit to the inevitable. However, he agreed to send Steyn's request to the British government. There was another meeting a few days later and the Boer leaders were presented to Milner. This academic administrator, who had never faced a bullet, thought the war should go on. He had already cabled Chamberlain to say that he did not trust the negotiations and considered that it would be more hopeful for the future if the war were allowed to continue until all the commandos had surrendered. The talks were then adjourned so that the commandants could return to their men to elect thirty representatives from each 'Republic'.

On 15 May the delegates met at Vereeniging on the border between the Transvaal and the Orange Free State. The discussions went on for days and three basic positions emerged: Botha, Smuts and De la Rey (who had been talked over by the other two) were in virtual agreement on terms of surrender; Hertzog, De Wet (and the absent Steyn) were holding out for independence; Milner was pushing for harsh terms, much to the annoyance of Kitchener, who was now virtually acting as a mediator between the two Boer parties. Late at night Smuts (though some authorities say it was Botha) had a talk with Kitchener, who expressed a private view that the Liberals would probably soon be in government and would then grant a constitution to South Africa. The message was taken back to the delegates and seems to have tipped the balance.

On the 23rd the meeting reassembled to hear a set of proposals drawn up by Milner in the form of a contract. This provided that if the burghers of both Republics surrendered, they and all prisoners who signed their allegiance to the British Crown would be allowed home. It also guaranteed that there would be an amnesty for all rebels, that Dutch would be taught in the schools and that Boers would be allowed to keep their rifles to protect their farms. A period of military rule would be followed by the development of civil government, and generous assistance would be given for reconstruction. The point which caused least contention, but which has plagued the country ever since, was that no decision should be made about the 'Native Franchise' until a representative constitution had been granted.

For a few days the Boers continued arguing. During this time Steyn's condition suddenly deteriorated and he had to be taken

122. The body of Commandant Potgieter on the battlefield.

home. His departure weakened the Free Staters' case, although De Wet, appointed acting President, continued to hold out for independence. On the afternoon of 31 May 1902, a vote was finally taken: forty-four delegates voted for, and six against, the acceptance of the surrender terms. The agreement was signed that night. Afterwards De la Rey walked on to the *stoep* of Kitchener's house and said in halting English to the dejected Boer leaders, 'We are a bloody cheerful-looking lot of British subjects!'[50]

All that remained was to break the news to the commandos who were anxiously waiting. On 2 June Kitchener made a speech of conciliation and the Boer chiefs left to talk to their men. Gradually the commandos rode in to surrender at the nearest military post. Most Boers signed the oath of allegiance to the British Crown, but some preferred exile to returning to their devastated farms. It took many weeks for the full impact of the destruction of farms and the concentration-camp deaths to be felt by the home-going men.

123. After the surrender

EPILOGUE

The war had as great an effect on Britain as it did on South Africa – perhaps greater in the long term. Britain's blunders in the field did not go unnoticed by the military attachés. Germany in particular was encouraged to step up the construction programme for the military machine which was to be used so successfully in 1914. But this story is not about Britain, so an attempt must be made to explain the most important long-term effect the war had on South Africa: it set the Boers on a political course which focused sharply on a single objective – to preserve their identity.

This was not immediately obvious during the first days after the Boer surrender. Reparations began immediately the fighting stopped. Milner and the 'kindergarten' of administrators he had collected round him worked like beavers to overcome the immediate problems. With the help of the Boer commando leaders they completed the resettlement very quickly. By the time the long-delayed rains came in 1903, the rebuilding programme was almost completed. Milner could now afford to concentrate on developing the country as a modern British colony. During the next few years things went so well under British rule that in May 1910 Lord Gladstone, the first Governor-General, proclaimed the unification of the four colonies into the Union of South Africa. Louis Botha became its first Prime Minister. Less than ten years after they had fought a major war against the British Empire and been defeated, the Boers were running one of Britain's wealthiest and most important colonies. An outsider could not be blamed for thinking that the Boer population were happy with the political arrangement, even though their independence had been taken from them.

But beneath this apparent harmony an undercurrent of discord was building up amongst the Boers that was to surface in the fiasco of the 1914 uprising. At the centre of the conflict was a confusion of leadership. Many Boers felt disappointed that Botha and Smuts had not held out against the British for better terms. The arguments of both men had been crucial in persuading the majority of Boer delegates at the peace negotiations to accept unconditional surrender. Now this began to count against them and they were seen as being too pro-British. Steyn and De Wet had held out for independence: this gave them credibility with the 'bitter-enders', who felt that all their efforts in the field and all the suffering in the concentration camps had gone for nothing. In the middle was the Transvaaler De la Rey: originally opposed to surrender, he had eventually been talked round by Smuts and Botha.

The only Boer leader with the authority to reconcile the two sides was Steyn: the old statesman who coined the phrase 'the bitter end' was the only pre-war politician to have proved his worth. But it soon became apparent that he was too ill for high office. Soon after Kitchener took over from Roberts in 1900 Steyn developed a mysterious illness which caused increasing weakness during each day, so that by the end he would be almost totally paralysed. It seems likely that he was suffering from myaesthenia gravis, a rare biochemical disease of the thymus gland which causes the muscles to become weaker the more they are used, until the patient cannot lift his arms or legs, or even open his eyes or swallow. Steyn's illness is certainly the reason why he did not become a key politician after the war.

With Steyn out of action, the 'triumvirate' of fighting commanders, Botha, De la Rey and De Wet, naturally assumed political leadership. At first their differences were held in check: De la Rey acted as mediator between Botha's inclination to achieve peace and harmony after a disastrous war and De Wet's militant determination to recreate the Republics. Although Botha's extraordinary ability to influence people and Smuts's fast talking had enabled them to prevail during the surrender talks, the hard-liners had reserved the right to try again at some time in the future when Britain got into difficulty. However, it was not long before both De la Rey and De Wet left the centre of the stage, and by 1910 a new voice had begun to dominate among the hard-liners with the emergence of General Hertzog as the strongest opponent of Botha's ideal of a united South African nation. The 1913 opening at Bloemfontein of the memorial to the Boer women who had died in the concentration camps also served to mobilize Afrikaner public opinion in favour of the hard-liners. This occasion was notable as the last on which all the Boer commanders were present together.

Meanwhile Smuts was content to serve British authority, and even began recruiting a South African army, the Union Defence Force. He appointed Christiaan Beyers as Commandant-General of the new army, with such die-hards as Kemp and Manie Maritz as staff officers. Behind Smuts's back they organized a country-wide plot to take over the government if the right opportunity occurred. When the outbreak of the First World War seized British attention, that moment seemed to have arrived. De la Rey called together a meeting of Boer leaders, who conceived the ill-fated plan of riding to Pretoria, collecting burghers as they went. De la Rey was sure that once Botha saw their overwhelming numbers they could persuade him to join them. But this discussion was never to take place. On 15 September De la Rey drove to Johannesburg. On the outskirts of the city his car was ordered to stop at a road-block by armed local police who had surrounded a gang of bank-robbers. De la Rey ordered the driver to go on. At the third road-block the police fired on the car and De la Rey was killed.

In the unrest that followed, De Wet, Maritz and Beyers led an open revolt against Britain, and, far from joining them, Botha and Smuts took the field against them. De Wet was captured and imprisoned and Beyers was drowned trying to escape across the Vaal River. Not only had the die-hards failed, they had suffered defeat at the hands of their former colleagues. Boer had fought Boer and the 'bitter-enders' had lost. The blow drove them almost underground, resulting in the formation of the Broederbond, a secret organization dedicated to preserving their language and culture and furthering the Afrikaner cause: they were not to surface again in strength until 21 years later.

But the events of the Boer War had guaranteed that Afrikaner nationalism would survive. In the early post-war years it was the memory of the camp deaths that drove Afrikaners together, but gradually the cruel reality of war gave way to the myths of a nation. It was easy to romanticize a grandfather who had trekked into the African interior by ox-wagon, had relied solely on his gun for survival, and for three years had checked the momentum of a whole empire. In those early years the movement took a linguistic form, with the refashioning of 'Kitchen Dutch' into what was now to be the Afrikaans language. Dictionaries were published, European classics translated, and a new Afrikaans literature emerged. English was systematically eliminated. It was an attempt to safeguard Afrikaners' individuality from what they saw as an all-pervasive 'Englishness' which had swallowed so many other nations which had come into contact with it.

Meanwhile, on the surface the process of conciliation seemed to be progressing satisfactorily. When Botha died unexpectedly in 1919, Smuts succeeded him as Prime Minister. Smuts's leadership of his party spanned four decades and many Afrikaners supported him, even Barry Hertzog, though he had reservations. In 1924 Hertzog became the first Nationalist Prime Minister, and in 1934 his party fused with that of Smuts as the United South African National Party, or United Party. Although Hertzog and others in the government were strongly in favour of a colour bar, particularly in industry and the mines, there were others such as Jan Hofmeyr who even advocated black franchise. However, these were not regarded as crucial issues at the time; there was more interest in the question of the fusion or separation of the English and Afrikaner elements of the population. Smuts's policy aimed at fusion, but even Hertzog came to agree with it and it gained

wide acceptance among Afrikaners. Gradually, however, the respect the Boers had felt for Smuts as a tough commandant was
eroded, and with it support for his policy of national unity. His
Cape background, his English education and his international interests had always been disliked; his wily intelligence inspired
mistrust; and, most damning of all, he was accused of lacking
Boer sentiment. But what finally drove most Afrikaners into the
Nationalist camp was his use of the army against Boer miners in
the 1922 strike. The centenary re-enactment of the Great Trek in
1938 was set up as a rallying point by the Broederbond, but even
they did not anticipate the extent of emotional fervour aroused by
the slow movement of the ox-wagons across the country. Many
more Afrikaners joined the 'cause'. Their triumph, so long in
preparation, finally came at the end of the Second World War,
when Smuts was ousted by a Nationalist party campaigning on a
platform of separate development free from British influence. It
seemed only natural that as well as rejecting British culture they
should set themselves 'apart' from black culture. They fought and
won the next and every subsequent election on the issue of
'apartheid'.

Today it is hard for anyone in Britain to conceive that South
African apartheid policies can in any way be a direct result of the
joint histories of the English and the Boers. Perhaps Steyn would
have found the end of the story more bitter even than he had
predicted.

NOTES

1. Unnamed reporter, quoted in Anon., *The Boer War* (R. E. King, London, 1900).

2. Letter from an unnamed lieutenant in the 1st King's Rifles, quoted in *The Boer War* (see n. 1).

3. Official Boer telegram: English translation in Volksraad Papers (1902).

4. Richard Ruda, 'The Irish Transvaal Brigades', *The Irish Sword*, Dublin, vol. xi (1973-4), pp. 201-11.

5. Unsigned letter accompanied by a covering letter suggesting that it was written by 'Higgins', who was a member of McBride's 1st Irish Brigade (MS 18138, John Devoy Papers, National Library of Ireland, Dublin).

6. Quoted in H. W. Wilson, *After Pretoria: The Guerilla War* (2 vols., Amalgamated Press, London, 1902), vol. ii. (This work was published as a Supplement to the same author's *With the Flag to Pretoria* [2 vols., Harmsworth Bros., London, 1900-1901] and presented as constituting vols. iii and iv of the earlier work.)

7. Sgt T. Secrett, *Twenty-five Years with Earl Haig* (Jarrold, London, 1929).

8. G. Lynch, *The Impressions of a War Correspondent* (George Newnes, London, 1903).

9. Sgt J. W. Lang, quoted in G. F. Gibson, *The Story of the Imperial Light Horse* (GD & Co., London, 1937).

10. L. S. Amery (gen. ed.), *The Times History of the War in South Africa* (7 vols., Sampson Low, Marston & Co., London, 1900-1909), vol. vi (ed. L. S. Amery).

11. From the diary of Major F. J. W. Porter, a surgeon in the RAMC. Published by permission of Mr M. Porter.

12. From an official report of 1902, 'History of No. 6 General Hospital from its Mobilization' (MS No. 480, Muniment Room, Royal Army Medical College, London).

13. From the diary of Major F. J. W. Porter (see n. 11).

14. ibid.

15. Entry for 18 February 1900 from Col. C. L. Veal, 'Diary of the Boer War', Part IV (MS 6810-19, National Army Museum, London).

16. From the diary of Major F. J. W. Porter (see n. 11).

17. ibid.

18. W. S. Churchill, *London to Ladysmith via Pretoria* (Longmans, Green & Co., London, 1900).

19. See J. Meintjies, *General Louis Botha* (Cassell, London, 1970).

20. Letter dated 27 January 1900 from Lieut.-Col. McCarthy O'Leary, South Lancs. Regiment, to the father of Frederick Raphael (Raphael Documents, National Army Museum, London).

21. Col. Sir John Hall, *The Coldstream Guards 1885–1914* (Oxford University Press, 1929).

22. G. Lynch, *The Impressions of a War Correspondent* (see n. 8).

23. C. R. de Wet, *The Three Years' War* (Constable & Co., London, 1902).

24. Telegram from De la Rey to Botha, quoted in M. Davitt, *The Boer Fight for Freedom* (Funk & Wagnall, New York and London, 1902).

25. M. Davitt, *The Boer Fight for Freedom* (see n. 24).

26. L. M. Phillipps, *With Rimington* (Edward Arnold, London, 1902).

27. Quoted in H. W. Wilson, *After Pretoria: The Guerilla War*, vol. i (vol. iii of *With the Flag to Pretoria*; see n. 6).

28. P. Pienaar, *With Steyn and De Wet* (Methuen, London, 1902).

29. Quoted in H. J. Ogden, *The War Against the Dutch Republics in South Africa: Its Origin, Progress, and Results* (National Reform Union Publications, London, 1901).

30. P. T. Ross, *A Yeoman's Letters* (Simpkin, Marshall, Hamilton, Keat & Co., London, 1901).

31. Anon., *The Oxfordshire Light Infantry in South Africa 1900–1901* (Eyre & Spottiswoode, 1901).

32. Trooper F. Perham, *The Kimberley Flying Column: Boer War Reminiscences* (pamphlet, Timaru, New Zealand, 1959).

33. ibid.

34. Lieut.-Col. L. E. L. du Moulin, *Two Years on Trek with the Royal Sussex Regiment* (Murray & Co., London, 1907).

35. P. T. Ross, *A Yeoman's Letters* (see n. 30).

36. See J. F. C. Fuller, *The Last of the Gentlemen's Wars* (Faber & Faber, London, 1937).

37. Circular Memorandum No. 29, from the Archives of the Military Governor, Pretoria, quoted in S. B. Spies, 'Roberts and Kitchener and Civilians in the Boer Republics, January 1900 to May 1902' (unpublished D.Phil. thesis, University of Witwatersrand, 1973).

38. L. H. Phillipps, *With Rimington* (see n. 26).

39. Adila Badenhorst, tr. E. Hobhouse, *Tant' Alie of Transvaal: Her Diary 1880–1902* (George Allen & Unwin, London, 1923).

40. F. Young, *Manchester Guardian*, quoted in the same author's *The Relief of Mafeking* (Methuen, London, 1900).

41. E. Neething, *Should We Forget?* (Holl.-Aff Publishing Co., Cape Town, 1920).

42. Quoted in S. B. Spies, unpublished thesis (see n. 37).

43. A. Badenhorst, *Tant' Alie of Transvaal* (see n. 39).

44. J. Brandt, *The Petticoat Commando, or Boer Women in the Secret Service* (Mills & Boon, London, 1913).

45. A. Badenhorst, *Tant' Alie of Transvaal* (see n. 39).

46. ibid.

47. *Women's Endurance* by A. D. L., Chaplain in the Concentration Camp, Bethulie, Orange River Colony, 1901 (Boer Relief Committee, Cape Town, 1904).

48. ibid.

49. L. S. Amery (gen. ed.), *The Times History of the War in South Africa* (see n. 10), vol. v (ed. E. Childers).

50. Quoted in T. O. Trevor, *Forty Years in Africa* (Hurst & Blackett, London, 1932).

DIARY OF EVENTS

October 1899

7th   British army mobilizes
10th   Boer ultimatum
12th   Boers invade Natal and Cape Colony
14th   Investment of Mafeking and Kimberley
20th   Battle of Talana Hill
21st   Battle of Elandslaagte Station
23rd   Battle of Dundee; death of General Penn Symons
30th   Battle of Ladysmith: siege begins
31st   Buller lands at Cape Town with army corps

November

Armoured train incident near Chieveley; Churchill captured
22nd   Buller leaves for Natal

BULLER'S CAMPAIGN

November

Advances of Boers in eastern Cape; Lord Methuen takes over
command of Orange River and commences his advance; arrival of
reinforcements of British troops, including the Canadian and Australian
contingents
23rd   Battle of Belmont
25th   Battle of Graspan
28th   Battle of Modder River

December

Black Week: three major defeats on:
10th   Battle of Stormberg
11th   Battle of Magersfontein
15th   Battle of Colenso
17th   Roberts appointed Commander-in-Chief; army reserve called out
23rd   Roberts and Kitchener leave England

ROBERTS'S MARCH

January 1900

Reorganization
10th   Arrival of Roberts in Cape Town
24th   Battle of Spionkop

February

5th   Battle of Vaalkrantz
12th   Roberts advances in Cape
15th   Relief of Kimberley
18th–27th   Battle of Paardeberg, culminating in surrender of Cronje
        with 4,000 Boers
28th   Buller relieves Ladysmith

March

7th   Battle of Poplar Grove
13th   Roberts captures Bloemfontein
31st   Battle of Sannah's Post

April

Delay at Bloemfontein; typhoid epidemic

May

3rd   Roberts advances from Bloemfontein
11th   Chamberlain announces intention to annexe Republics
17th   Relief of Mafeking
24th   Annexation of the Orange Free State
31st   Capture of Johannesburg

June

5th   Capture of Pretoria
11th   Battle of Diamond Hill

July

4th   Roberts and Buller join hands
30th   Prinsloo surrenders at Brandwater Basin
Scattered fighting in spite of captured Boers signing
Oath; Roberts authorizes burning of farms used by 'guerilla
fighters'; start of 'First De Wet Hunt'

September

1st   Annexation of Transvaal
11th   Kruger leaves for Europe
24th   British reach Mozambican border at Komatipoort

GUERILLA WAR

October

 8th   Milner appointed administrator of new colonies
19th   Kruger leaves Lourenço Marques for Marseilles
24th   Buller returns to England

November

16th   De Wet tries to invade Cape Colony
23rd   De Wet captures Dewetsdorp
29th   Kitchener succeeds Roberts as Commander-in-Chief

December

 5th   De Wet forced to abandon attempt to enter Cape
11th   Lord Roberts leaves South Africa
14th   De Wet and Steyn escape from hunting columns
16th   Commandos under Kritzinger and Hertzog enter Cape
20th   Martial law proclaimed in northern Cape

January 1901

 1st   Colonial Defence Force called out in Cape Colony
4th–31st   Attacks by De la Rey, Beyers, De Wet and Smuts

February

 7th   30,000 additional mounted troops dispatched to South Africa
10th   De Wet enters Cape Colony
13th   Kitchener proposes peace meeting to Botha
19th   De Wet chased out of Cape
28th   Milner moves headquarters to Johannesburg

March

16th   Botha refuses Kitchener's peace terms

April

10th   Elliot begins major drives in Free State

May/June

Drives continue; Kritzinger and Scheepers active

July

Major drives in Cape Colony

August

 7th   Kitchener proclaims banishment for Boer leaders captured
       armed after 15 September

September

  3rd   Smuts invades Cape Colony
  5th   Commandant Lotter captured
  7th   Botha attempts to invade Natal
17th   Successful attacks by Smuts, De la Rey and Botha

October

Capture of troops and supply convoys continues
  9th   Martial Law extended in Cape
11th   Commandant Lotter executed; Commandant Scheepers captured

November

Major drives continue in Free State and Transvaal
29th   De Wet attacks convoy near Speyfontein

December

  7th   National Scout Corps inaugurated
16th   Kritzinger captured
17th   Johannesburg Stock Exchange reopened
23rd   Blockhouse line between Kroonstad and Lindley completed
25th   De Wet captures Tweefontein camp

January 1902

  4th   Defeat of British unit near Ermelo
10th   German Chancellor makes anti-British speech in Reichstag
17th   Commandant Scheepers executed at Graaff Reinet
29th   British government refuses Dutch government's offer to mediate

February

  5th   Convoy captured near Beaufort West
  6th   New 'De Wet Hunt' begins in Free State
  7th   De Wet breaks through blockhouse line

March

  7th   Lord Methuen wounded and captured at Tweebosch
24th   Major drive begins in western Transvaal
26th   Rhodes dies in Cape Town

April

  4th   Smuts invests O'kiep
  6th   Kritzinger acquitted of murder charges
  9th   Boer peace delegates meet at Klerksdorp

May

15th   Opening of Vereeniging conference
18th   Boer delegates meet Kitchener and Milner at Pretoria
31st   Surrender document signed

GLOSSARY

Afrikaans: the language used today by descendants of the Dutch in South Africa

Afrikander: Dutch word used after the Great Trek for Dutch settlers who remained in the Cape Colony

Afrikaner: current name used for descendants of Dutch colonists in South Africa

apartheid: separateness

berg: mountain

bitter-ender: Boer fighter who remained in the field to the end of the Boer War

Boer: lit. 'farmer'; the name applied to Dutch colonists who left the Cape during the Great Trek and set up two republics in the interior

bos-veld: bush country covered in undergrowth and trees

burgher: male citizen of the Boer Republics

bywoner: itinerant farmer living on someone else's farm and paying with his labour

commandant: senior officer in charge of commando

Commandant-General: commander of the army

commandeer: to obtain supplies for a commando from local inhabitants; government vouchers were usually given in payment

commando: Boer regiment

donga: cutting made in the ground by water

dorp: village

drift: ford across a river

Kaffir: from the Arabic for 'infidel'; term used by British and Boers for South African blacks; now extremely offensive

kop: lit. 'head'; hill

koppie: diminutive of *kop*; small hill

kraal: black village; group of huts; cattle enclosure

kriegsraad: Boer tactical meeting before battle

laager: camp; during the Great Trek often formed by a circle of ox-wagons

nek: pass between two hills

poort: 'gate'; used in town names; also break or gap between hills

spruit: watercourse, often dry

trek: (v.) to move, travel; (n.) movement of people, journey

trek-Boer: farmer looking for new land; origin of the name 'Boer' (q.v.)

Uitlanders: lit. 'foreigners'; the name given by the Boers to foreigners who came to live in the Johannesburg mining areas

vegt-general, or *vecht-general:* general or commander in the field
veld: open country, as opposed to town
veld-cornet: junior officer
verkenner: military scout
Volksraad: Boer parliament
ZARPS: South African police

PHOTOGRAPHIC ACKNOWLEDGEMENTS

The author and publishers are grateful to the following for permission to reproduce photographs in this book:

Africana Museum, Johannesburg: 1, 22, 25, 27, 29, 31, 53, 58, 109, 117, 120, 122; Boer War Museum, Bloemfontein: 20, 51, 52, 71, 105, 106, 107, 111, 112, 119a, 119b; Cape Town Archives: 121; Kodak Museum, Hendon: 3, 4, 5, 41, 63, 79, 96; Local History Museum, Durban: 16; National Army Museum, Chelsea: 6, 9, 10, 13, 18, 37, 47, 61, 76, 83, 92, 93, 101, 104, 119c; National Museum of Ireland: 30, 32; RAMC Library, Millbank: 46, 73, 102, 113, 114; Transvaal State Archives, Pretoria: 42, 55, 72; Underwood & Underwood: 2, 11, 12, 17, 36, 60, 67, 68, 69; Lord Methuen's Collection: 40, 43, 44, 45, 50, 54, 59, 64, 66, 75, 85, 90; Richard Cobb Collection: 94, 108, 110, 115; A. Speyer Collection: 38, 39; William Gordon Davis: 56.

All other photographs are from the author's personal collection.

INDEX